THE LONG RANGE DESERT GROUP

DEDICATION

This book is dedicated to William 'Swede' Anderson, Toby Savage and Nigel Hirst - three men who were instrumental in the development of this book.

THE LONG RANGE DESERT GROUP

HISTORY & LEGACY

Karl-Gunnar Norén & Lars Gyllenhaal

Helion & Company

Helion & Company Limited
Unit 8 Amherst Business Centre
Budbrooke Road
Warwick
CV34 5WE
England
Tel. 01926 499 619
Fax 0121 711 4075
Email: info@helion.co.uk
Website: www.helion.co.uk
Twitter: @helionbooks
Visit our blog http://blog.helion.co.uk/

Published by Helion & Company 2019
Designed and typeset by Battlefield Design, Gloucester (www.battlefield-design.co.uk)
Cover designed by Paul Hewitt, Battlefield Design (www.battlefield-design.co.uk)
Printed by Gutenberg Press Limited, Tarxien, Malta

Text © Karl-Gunnar Norén & Lars Gyllenhaal 2019
Photographs © as individually credited
Cover photograph by John Carroll
Maps drawn by and © Stig Söderlind 2019

ISBN 978-1-911628-88-0

British Library Cataloguing-in-Publication Data.
A catalogue record for this book is available from the British Library.

For details of other military history titles published by Helion & Company
Limited contact the above address, or visit our website: http://www.helion.co.uk.

We always welcome receiving book proposals from prospective authors.

Contents

List of Photographs

In Colour Section

List of Maps

Maps in Colour Section

Acknowledgements

The authors would like to cordially thank the Churchill Archives Centre at Churchill College as well as the Long Range Desert Group Preservation Society, the Royal Signals Museum, the Alexander Turnbull Library at the National Library of New Zealand, Archives New Zealand and the following individuals for their valuable help:

Erik Ahlström
Peter Anderson
William "Swede" Anderson
Bob Atwater
John Carroll
David Hall
Lena Kamhed
Mahmud Marai
Olga Nielsen
Göran Norén
Mikael Norman
James D. Patch
Jason Paterniti
Rick Pewé
David C. Retter
Toby Savage
Alan & Shelley Seay
Christine Seymour
Christer Sjölin
Martin Skipworth
Hans Strelow
Stig Söderlind
Jack Valenti
Sam Watson

Preface

In 2002 the Special Air Service (SAS) memorial was opened in Scotland near the family estate of SAS founder David Stirling. In 2014 a large stone was added to the memorial, bearing the scorpion badge of the Long Range Desert Group (LRDG) and the words "THEY SHOWED THE WAY". The addition was paid for by the SAS Regimental Association. Why did veterans of the SAS, the world´s most famous special forces unit, decide to add those words? Well, that is something this book will explain.

Why did we, two Swedes, write this book? In our opinion the LRDG was the Second World War´s most innovative unit and unusually successful. After 1945 the unit got some acknowledgement in the UK and in New Zealand. However, not as much credit as it deserved, and in the Second World War histories of other countries it is often not even mentioned. We, the authors of this book, are from such a country. But, as we will demonstrate, even our native Sweden in a way contributed to the LRDG, by way of some anti-tank guns.

The guns and other weapons used in the Second World War are now largely fit only for museums, but many of the LRDG´s inventions and experiences are still valid and will remain so. Not least their survival skills, desert driving techniques and vehicle modifications. We have tested some of the 'LRDG lessons' and wish to make them better known for the benefit of modern long range travellers.

Our book is based on our LRDG book collections, correspondence with two of the veterans and visits to LRDG-founder Ralph Bagnold´s archive in Cambridge. Add to this our own experiences in Libya and Egypt. There is more about our sources later on, as well as everyone who has contributed to this book.

We wish to immediately recognize a deficiency. This book does not portray the full hell of war. However, the war in North Africa – the main theatre of operations of the LRDG – to a great extent differed from the Second World War in Europe and Asia. In North Africa relatively few civilians were bombed, shot dead or persecuted. Also, in the LRDG very few men, amazingly few, were killed – why that is the case can be explained by the stealthy and smart nature of the unit.

Another reason one might call the war in North Africa 'less evil' is that for Egypt, Libya and Tunisia it accelerated their decolonization. Thus it was a step towards their independence. Our perhaps naive hope is that in the future it will be safer to visit these countries and that this book will inspire you to go there yourself.

Karl-Gunnar Norén and Lars Gyllenhaal

Part One

North Africa 1939-1943

"In my view the LRDG was the finest of all units serving in the desert."
Sir David Stirling, founder of the Special Air Service

"The more I saw of the LRDG, the more impressed I was [...] The desert, particularly that part of it which was nominally enemy territory, became a second home to them."
Sir Fitzroy Maclean, early SAS officer

1

A Man Called Bagnold

When travelling as a passenger on a spacious and comfortable ocean liner towards a distant harbour one gets many opportunities to think and reminisce. What did the 43-year-old British Major Ralph Bagnold ponder when he gazed at the endless sea from the former cruise ship *Franconia* in October 1939? We can safely assume that his thoughts were never far from sand. The North African desert had been his burning passion during the interwar years. He had just finished writing a major study about the physics of blowing sand. He had spent no less than five years writing it. He described his hobby, even after his highly successful desert war years, as "rather useless".[1] But perhaps those words were mostly a sign of his sense of humour.

Now he was on his way to Africa again. Not to his beloved Egypt or Libya, but at least to the right continent. The new world war was just one month old and he was en route to Kenya, to which the British Army in its infinite wisdom had chosen to send him.

His looks were the result of years of physical and mental strain in places so desolate that not a single soul had seen them before him.[2] But, as the hardships had been totally voluntary, he did not simply look weatherworn. Even from afar you could see he was a fit man. Aside from a large moustache his face was dominated by a pair of calm, friendly eyes.

His last name, Bagnold, was of very dusty Anglo-Saxon origin. His first name, Ralph, matched the athletic and decent impression that he radiated.

His moustache was just like those on the recruiting posters of 1914-18 and, indeed, Bagnold had served in the Great War. He had joined the Royal Engineers and fought in France. His first wish after having survived the hell of the trenches was to study at Cambridge and become a civil engineer. After Cambridge he nevertheless rejoined the army, perhaps it was in his genes. His father, a colonel, had been part of the great Nile expedition to save General Gordon in Sudan.

Back in His Majesty's service Ralph Bagnold was stationed in India in an area not far from Afghanistan, and thereafter in Cairo. In 1922 Egypt was formally recognized by the United Kingdom as an independent state but, in practice, there were still strong bonds with London. Cairo was at the time the premier city of exotic night life, but what Bagnold appreciated with the city was finding several fellow exploration companions among the younger British officers. Instead of indulging in nocturnal activities this fellowship preferred to challenge the desert and themselves by undertaking very long range car trips.[3]

The ordinary cars of the time, especially the American ones, were rather well suited for poor road conditions, or even off-road, as roads actually made for cars were still quite scarce.

---

1   Ralph Bagnold, 'The Early Days of the Long Range Desert Group', *The Geographical Journal*, Vol.105, No.1/2, (Jan-Feb 1945), pp. 30-42.
2   Ralph Bagnold, *Libyan Sands: Travel in a Dead World* (London: Eland, 2010). This book was the very first one that LRDG Association secretary Jim Patch recommended to Lars Gyllenhaal, in his first letter to Gyllenhaal, dated 3 August 1985. The letter is in the LRDG collection of Gyllenhaal.
3   Bagnold (2010), p. 13.

The band of motoring friends would drive to Palestine and Jordan. They would even drive as far as India to purchase a new vehicle. What was it that so attracted Bagnold and his friends? The pyramids, especially the ones only just discovered, of course, were part of the story. But even more they wanted to enter whole areas totally uncharted, landscapes not yet documented anywhere. In addition, the expeditions turned into a sort of sport, a new British team sport. The preparations for the trips were challenging and exciting in themselves, and a part which Bagnold really loved about them. This is quite apparent from reading *Libyan Sands*, his inspiring account of how he became such a fanatic about the desert.[4]

Bagnold and his companions searched for mysterious places like the ancient legendary city of Zerzura. The group of friends evolved into the 'Zerzura club'.[5] Among the hardcore desert enthusiasts nationality was secondary. Thus not only Brits could join the desert pioneers, but also the infamous Hungarian Count László Almásy – today known as 'The English Patient' because of the well-known motion picture. In his mind, Zerzura was not just one of several enchanted places he wanted to find. He seemed to be haunted by the thought that the magical city was yet to be rediscovered (there still exists a fascination with Zerzura, linking it to the most deranged parts of the Nazi SS). Bagnold had a more sober attitude towards Zerzura and became sure that it was only a good story, an inspiration.[6] But, while searching for Zerzura, he did learn a number of tricks - enabling him to venture further and further into the hot heart of the desert. He passed dunes that had previously been considered impassable regardless of the chosen mode of transportation.

Ralph Bagnold was the driving force behind these pioneering voyages and through them he was able to create many of the very down to earth principles that he would later use in his struggle against the desert forces of Benito Mussolini and Adolf Hitler.

Formally, Bagnold was an amateur scientist, but the word amateur was quite misleading, since from early on he was equally serious in his research methods as real, reputable scientists.

However, the 1930s caused such financial strain that Bagnold was forced to seek a civilian livelihood. But, when the new world war broke out, he was obliged to again don a uniform, he was called up. He had no problem with that, but why on earth to Kenya? He disliked having to fight in a country which he knew almost nothing about. He also knew that to protest about it would hardly pay off.

A Historical Collision

During its journey through the Mediterranean the *Franconia* collided with another troop ship, the *Alcantara*. This freak accident proved to be crucial for Bagnold.[7] The vessels could barely make it to Malta, where Bagnold was ordered to board a new ship. He was told that he would no longer travel straight through the Suez Canal to Mombasa, Kenya. He would have to first spend some time in Port Said, Egypt...

Bagnold was only due to stay in Egypt for a few days and then proceed to Kenya. But a reporter happened to catch sight of him, and not just any reporter, but one who many years before had got to know Bagnold because of his extreme desert hobby. The result of this chance encounter was this small but, as it turned out, highly significant piece in the *Egyptian Gazette*:

4   Bagnold (2010).
5   Saul Kelly, *The Lost Oasis: The True Story Behind The English Patient* (Boulder: Westview Press, 2003), p. 1.
6   Bagnold (2010), p. 216.
7   Bagnold (2010), p. 219.

Ralph Bagnold during the First World War.
(Churchill Archives Centre, Ralph Bagnold,
BGND, C12)

Bagnold, the explorer and
researcher. Photo from
1945 or shortly after.
(Royal Signals Museum)

Major Bagnold's presence in Egypt at this time seems a reassuring indication that one of the cardinal errors of 1914-18 is not to be repeated. During that war, if a man had made a name for himself as an explorer of Egyptian deserts, he would almost certainly have been sent to Jamaica to report on the possibilities of increasing rum production [...]. Nowadays, of course, everything is done much better.[8]

Especially the last sentence signaled that Bagnold had actually not been stationed in Egypt. This camouflaged criticism was noted by the regional British military leadership, headed by General Archibald Wavell. He had until recently been working in a tiny office writing long lists, purely theoretical, in preparation for an outbreak of war. The British government worked hard to try to keep Italy out of the war, as it would be quite enough having to fight against Germany. Consequently, nothing was done on the ground to possibly disturb the relations between Egypt and Libya. But in case things got worse, given that Germany and Italy were already allies, the British forces at least needed a plan.

Shortly after those words in the *Egyptian Gazette* had been published, Bagnold was called to the headquarters for BTE, British Troops Egypt. He had been looking forward to meeting some of his old comrades, when he stepped into the headquarters. Once there, he learned that General Wavell himself wanted to meet him. In spite of his desert skills he was somewhat surprised. A general meeting him? Was he not just a major in the reserves?

The conversation with General Wavell, often as taciturn as Bagnold, went something like this:

- Good morning Bagnold. I know about you. You have been stationed in Kenya. Do you know anything about that country?

- No, sir.

- More useful here, correct?

- Yes, sir.

- Good. That's all for now.[9]

Immediately after that brief conversation, Bagnold's posting was changed to the motorised unit in Mersa Matruh under General Percy 'Hobo' Hobart.[10] This unit was later to become the 7th Armoured Division, the original Desert Rats.

General Wavell had a special feeling about Bagnold, most probably because he was aware of the pioneering desert operations of the Light Car Patrols of 1916-19.[11] In addition he had met T.E. Lawrence, better known as Lawrence of Arabia, who was something of a counterpart to Bagnold during the First World War.[12] His conversations with Lawrence on irregular warfare had made a deep impression on him. Bagnold had, of course, corresponded with Lawrence.

The day after the conversation with the general, Bagnold stepped aboard the train to Mersa Matruh, a garrison town situated about halfway between Alexandria and the Libyan border.

At this time, the autumn of 1939, the new world war was still mainly in the Phoney War phase, the strange initial period of the war that was without major military actions between the Western Allies and Germany. The Soviet attack on Finland in November, a result of the pact between Hitler and Stalin, proved that war in Europe was real enough – and even led to the formation of a British

8   David Lloyd Owen, *Providence Their Guide: The Long Range Desert Group 1940-1945* (Barnsley: Pen & Sword, 2000), p. 6.

9   Ralph Bagnold, *Sand, Wind, and War: Memoirs of a Desert Explorer* (Tucson: University of Arizona Press, 1991), p. 123; Lloyd Owen, p. 6.

10   Lloyd Owen, p. 6.

11   W.B. Kennedy Shaw, *Long Range Desert Group: The story of its work in Libya* (London: Collins, 1945), p. 15; Robin Jenner & David List, *The Long Range Desert Group* (London: Osprey Publishing Ltd., 1985), p. 4.

12   Kelly, p. 158; Kennedy Shaw, p. 26.

Expeditionary Force to Finland, with the future SAS founder David Stirling as one of its members.[13] But, rather amazingly, a showdown between the major armies was still several months away.

Egypt was at this stage far from most European minds, but, with its strategic Suez Canal, the country was of growing interest to some Axis generals.

A New Map

A ship collision and a newspaper notice had thus placed Bagnold on the border with Libya, and here he began to process the recent big news. Within him formed a new geopolitical map that was frightening to behold. During the previous world war, Italy and Great Britain had been allies. Now a different Italy, Fascist Italy, had a quarter of a million troops in Libya. Fascist ambitions had just been exposed by Mussolini's invasion of Abyssinia (Ethiopia's name at the time).[14] Italian troops were thus stationed both west and south of Egypt. Moreover, Italy had signed a pact with the Third Reich, that was formally at war with Britain.

To be precise, Italian troops were now present in a series of Libyan oases with desert forts, all the way down to 'Uneiwat on the Sudanese border. The distance between 'Uweinat and the large Aswan Dam in Egypt was 800 kilometres. That may sound quite far away, but the terrain in between was mostly flat as a pancake. Even standard trucks could probably traverse that area. The specialist desert unit the Italians possessed since a decade - that Ralph Bagnold himself had encountered - would easily reach the Nile. Neither Egyptians nor British, however, had the capacity to even notice an incursion in the area before the conquest of the Aswan Dam would be a fact. The only really useful formation in the region that the British then had was the weak tank division in which Bagnold was serving as a signals officer. But it was in the other end of Egypt.

Now Bagnold began developing his thoughts on a light and mobile force that could both reconnoiter and disrupt enemy activities far behind the front line.

Since there at the time existed no British army vehicles suitable for extreme desert expeditions, Bagnold began experimenting with a half-dozen different civilian trucks.[15] It all culminated in a proposal he submitted to his boss General Percy Hobart. The latter had already damaged his career opportunities by proposing extensive motorization of the army, and he realized, of course, the wisdom of Bagnold's proposal, and promised to forward it to the top. This in spite of that his superiors would probably reject it, which he also warned about.[16] And he was right.

The War Office indeed declined to accept the wisdom of Bagnold's proposal. In essence it showed he had already figured out the basic recipe for what later became the Long Range Desert Group.[17] He envisioned a new patrol organisation with American vehicles, and how the patrols must be able to cross the sand seas, operate for two weeks without support and be sufficiently well armed to take out enemy escort units.

Already at this time Bagnold was also well aware of the Italian trick of creating a system of subterranean petrol and water depots. Likewise, he knew that desert patrol vehicles ideally should be combined with light aircraft and that the main threat to long range patrols would be hostile aircraft – making camouflage and dispersal vital.

---

13   Alan Hoe, *David Stirling* (London: Warner Books, 1994), p. 45.
14   Swedish officers in Ethiopian service stayed put when Mussolini invaded and this fact partly explains why the country was not immediately knocked out by the Italian ground and air force units. For more about these officers see Lars Gyllenhaal & Lennart Westberg, *Swedes at War: Willing Warriors of a Neutral Nation* (Bedford: The Aberjona Press, 2010), pp. 76-82.
15   Jenner & List, p. 9.
16   Lloyd Owen, p. 7.
17   Ibid; Gavin Mortimer, *The Men Who Made the SAS* (London: Constable, 2015:1), p. 16.

Bagnold also knew that the logical first task would be choosing the right vehicle, then to gather a core group of capable and trustworthy people. Then test both loads and performance, make decisions about armament and equipment.

In short, Bagnold was a man who had a clear idea of what ought to be done. But London - and thus Cairo - at this time (late 1939) did not investigate Bagnold's farsighted proposals. Mussolini might somehow be provoked. But that was only one reason. The second was a deep ignorance of the desert. Would not such patrols just get lost and disappear? Camel units with Bedouins might make it over those huge dunes, possibly. Bagnold's proposal to send motorized patrols across the Great Sand Sea was just not feasible, the leading generals thought. Bagnold was probably deranged.[18] Like his eccentric boss Percy Hobart, who wanted to replace horses with armoured vehicles and always had unconventional ideas.[19]

Shortly thereafter, Hobart was sacked. Bagnold tried, again, with his successor, to get support for his ideas. Again a positive response, but the end result was the same.

But Bagnold did at least get a transfer to Cairo and was thus able to get a better understanding of the situation, not least by visiting the classic Shepheard's Hotel, where all diplomats, reporters and spies had a drink or two. There you could catch the latest rumors and during the first war years the gist was often that there were many people, both Egyptians and other nationalities, who wanted the British out, and would gladly welcome the Italians and Germans as liberators.

After the fall of France came Italy's not very bold war entry, on 10 June 1940. Perhaps the British army was now more receptive to Ralph Bagnold's vision? General Wavell, the one who realized the sense in letting Bagnold stay in Egypt, was now not only the most senior British general in Cairo, but also the head of a new military command that stretched all the way from the Burmese border to West Africa and from the Balkans to South Africa. Wavell's headquarters therefore had both been given a new name, GHQ Middle East, and new fresh forces from Britain. Several of the stuffier officers had been swept away. The atmosphere was totally changed.

When Bagnold again met Wavell there were some pleasant surprises. The general had not only understood that Bagnold was a unique asset thanks to the immense desert knowledge he had gained through his odd hobby, Wavell also fully recognized the need for reconnaissance units of the model Ralph wanted to create.[20]

There was also no longer any doubt that a real crisis was coming. It was only a matter of time before Italian General Graziani's 15 divisions in Libya would roll across the border heading for the Nile and the Suez Canal.[21] And there was not that much that could stop either them or the Duke of Aosta and his Italian forces in Abyssinia (Ethiopia). Wavell's combined forces were only one-tenth as large. In addition, reinforcements across the Mediterranean were no longer possible. Now they would have to sail via the Cape of Good Hope.

How about some piracy?

When Bagnold through an adjutant of the general managed to place a copy of his plan on the general's table, it took less than an hour before he was in front of Wavell.[22] The conversation probably sounded something like this:

18   Bagnold (2010), p. 220.
19   Mortimer (2015:1), p. 16.
20   Lloyd Owen, p. 8.
21   Churchill Archives Centre (CAC): Ralph Bagnold, BGND C 13 (vol II): 'THE WORK OF THE LONG RANGE DESERT GROUP' dated 12 February 1941.
22   Bagnold (2010), p. 220.

- Tell us about your plans, Bagnold. How would you get inside Libya?

- Straight through the Great Sand Sea, sir. It is the most unlikely place. Just west of Ain Dalla.

- What would you do on the other side?

- Find the routes to both Kufra Oasis and 'Uweinat and read the tracks to get an idea of traffic, direction of travel, vehicle types, sir.

- What are the risks?

- Two, sir. The weather is one, nobody knows how hot it will get, no Europeans have been there in summer. The second is the map on your desk, sir. The passage of the Great Sand Sea is printed on it, and the map has been for sale in Cairo for years.

- What about the tracks, Bagnold? They are there for many years?

- Yes, in some desert terrain it is so.[23] But it is very difficult to follow tracks from the air. Planes fly too fast. If the tracks suddenly go sideways one loses sight of them. And the tracks on the dunes disappear with the first wind.

- What would you do if you were to find no signs of unusual activity?

- How about some piracy on the high desert?[24]

At this point Wavell went silent for at least half a minute, and Bagnold feared he had gone too far, been irreverent. All that was heard was the fan's futile attempts to keep the heat away. But then there was a reaction:

- Can you be ready in six weeks?

- Yes, provided...

- Any questions?

- Personnel and equipment, sir.

- Of course there´ll be opposition and delay.

Wavell then pressed a button, and instead of an adjutant, his chief of staff, General Sir Arthur Smith, came in. "Arthur," said Wavell, "Bagnold seeks a talisman. Get this typed for my signature right away: To all heads of departments and branches. I wish any request by Major Bagnold in person to be met at once without question. Wavell, Supreme Commander GHQ Middle East."[25]

With the Italian declaration of war every British unit in Egypt was holding on to all available vehicles, spare parts and equipment. To get a document of the above kind was thus no small miracle. Bagnold did not waste a second but started to make use of it the very same afternoon.[26]

Regarding personnel, unfortunately just about everyone Bagnold really knew and trusted in the army was far away. His old friend and desert travel companion in Cairo, Rupert Harding-Newman, was the exception. He came to serve as a liaison with the Egyptian military, who were officially not part of the war. A most faithful participant in many interwar desert adventures had been Guy Prendergast, but he was still in the UK. Another friend of Bagnold´s, archaeologist, botanist and navigator Bill Kennedy Shaw, was at the time a museum curator in Jerusalem and needed time to get free. What about good old Pat Clayton then? The man who had spent nearly twenty years with the Egyptian Survey, mapping large areas of previously unmapped desert. Well, he was on a surveying job somewhere in the Tanganyika wastelands, hard to even contact.[27]

---

23   "In places in the Egyptian deserts the old tracks of the car patrols of 1916 can still be plainly seen.". Source: CAC: Ralph Bagnold, BGND C 13 (vol II): 'THE WORK OF THE LONG RANGE DESERT GROUP' dated 12 February 1941, p. 3.

24   This and the previous sentence are the exact words in Bagnold (2010), p. 221.

25   Bagnold (2010), p. 221.

26   Official approval from General Wavell came on 23 June 1940. See e.g. *Special Forces in the Desert War 1940-43* (Kew: The National Archives, 2008), p. 14.

27   Tanganyika is today part of Tanzania.

However, in a miraculous manner, both Kennedy Shaw and Clayton succeeded in coming to the rescue faster than expected.[28] Both were made captains under Bagnold, and became instrumental for the new and very unconventional unit.[29]

Now Bagnold "only" had to create a fully motorized desert unit. Starting with zero vehicles.

28   Kennedy Shaw, p. 16.
29   Mike Morgan, *Sting of the Scorpion* (Stroud, The History Press, 2010).

2

Desert Vehicles and Weapons

Ralph Bagnold rejected the British Army's standard vehicles for more than one good reason. They were high and difficult to camouflage in the desert. They also had substandard abilities in the shifting desert terrain. Bagnold had already tested and compared many vehicles. He was grateful that he had just been given a free hand to choose vehicles and weapons.

Every pound mattered. Only the bare minimum could be carried to enable the desired radius. Therefore Bagnold chose two-wheel drive (2WD) cars. That might seem really weird, but four-wheel drive (4WD) meant more mechanics and thus increased weight, plus higher fuel consumption. More mechanical parts also meant more things that could break down – and there were of course limited possibilities for repairs in the desert.

The unit's first vehicles thus were civilian Chevrolet trucks, but, as it turned out, with some remarkable military qualities. Most were Chevrolet WBs and they were all 30-cwt, the latter three letters meaning the load capacity of the vehicle measured in hundredweight.[1] Translated to the metric system the load capacity was 1.5 tonnes.

To go outside the system and purchase civilian products turned out to be quite easy, thanks to Wavell's magical order. Bagnold bought as many Chevrolets he could get his hands on, from a local car dealer, adding a few from army stores. Bagnold now had a total of 14 trucks. They had chassis and cabs but lacked loading platforms. Then he managed to borrow 19 trucks from the Egyptian Army. In total, he had by September 1940 scraped together 33 Chevrolet 30-cwt trucks, to serve as the standard desert patrol vehicle, plus four Ford 15-cwt pickups that would serve as command vehicles.[2]

All vehicles were gathered in the Army workshops. Here Bagnold talked intensively with the foremen, unfurled sketches and pointed out details. He could motivate his ideas by experiences of many cars during his desert expeditions since the mid-1920s. The workshop men followed his instructions and cut off the roof and windshields of cabs. Such things, as well as doors, were mostly unnecessary out in the desert and were thus an unwanted weight. Free view in all directions also meant a better chance to detect enemy aircraft. Freedom of movement was also very useful for the machine gunners and when using the vital sun compass (more on that piece of kit later).

The workshops also built more practical steel bodies, with plenty of room for jerry cans, rations, radios and sand channels. The latter to "unstick" vehicles stuck in the sand.

---

1   Jenner & List, p. 9; Tim Moreman, *Long Range Desert Group Patrolman* (Oxford: Osprey Publishing Ltd, 2010), p. 27.
2   *Special Forces in the Desert War 1940-43*, p. 16.

The LRDG workhorses

The first patrol vehicles were commercial Chevrolet 30-cwt trucks. To allow for heavier loads extra blades were added to the springs. The normal windshields were replaced with much smaller ones, similar to those on aircraft – also part of the distinctive "LRDG look".

Because of extreme wear, the two-wheel drive Chevrolet WB had to be replaced with the four-wheel drive Ford CMP F30 30-cwt. Gasoline consumption thus increased drastically, and therefore the operational radius was halved. Ford V8 engines were also significantly more sensitive to sand, and oil consumption soared. When the LRDG used these vehicles the bonnets were usually removed, for better cooling, and the condenser was placed on the footboard.

However, the Ford CMP F30 was largely replaced in March 1942, because no less than 200 specially ordered Chevrolets model 1533X2 30-cwt then started arriving. This virtually perfect LRDG vehicle was actually a rather common right-hand drive 1.5 tonne lorry without roof and doors, modified according to Bagnold's specifications by General Motors of Canada. It was a stable construction and proved to be incredibly reliable. It has become the vehicle type most associated with the LRDG. There are reports of vehicles performing somersaults but still functioning mechanically after knocking out the dents. During a raid Captain Nick Wilder rammed a tank at full speed to give the rest of his patrol safe passage. Although his Chevrolet was properly beat up, he could continue his journey and reach safety.[3]

Each vehicle had several mounts for machine guns: mounts to shoot forwards and backwards, as well as against attacking aircraft. Plus mounts along the body sides for firing at parallel convoys – hostile ones that is.

The regular road tyres were exchanged for desert tyres. As these were wider, the fenders had to be widened.

Inventions

LRDG vehicles (later not only LRDG) also received some very ingenious contraptions to conserve water, based on a forgotten idea from the First World War refined and used by Ralph Bagnold during his hobby expeditions. As opposed to normal water cooling systems which allowed boiling water to evaporate through a vent on top of the radiator, Bagnold placed a pipe on top of that vent, collecting the steam and directing it to an external container where it condensed back to water. As the engine cooled, pressure in the radiator would drop and the water from the external container would be sucked back into the cooling system. The success of the device depended on the driver being able to tell when the water in the radiator was boiling over. When it had been boiling for some time, the water in the can was also brought to the boil, and steam issued from a vent hole in its top. The driver had to stop at this moment, or better just before it. Otherwise water would be lost by coming up through the vent hole. The driver then had to turn his vehicle into the wind, and wait for a few minutes. After a while the condensation of steam in the radiator had created enough vacuum to suck water automatically back out of the can into the radiator, provided there was no

3   Bart Vanderween, 'Desert Chevrolets: A lone Long Range Desert Group survivor and its contemporaries', *Wheels & Tracks* No. 8 (July 1984), pp. 14-21.

INSTRUCTIONS

For   use   of   Bagnold   Sun-Compass

TO ALIGN.   See that plane of compass is parallel to that of ground on which vehicle stands (vehicle ready loaded for journey and clamping nut loose). Aim vehicle at a distant object. Turn whole compass till side pointer and adjusting thumb-screw are both to the rear: and pointer, central needle and distant object are accurately in line. Tighten clamping nut.

TO SET.

I. Solar Time.   Select the appropriate column of the Azimuth Card. Alter watch from Standard Time; (a) by the given correction for the Equation of Time; and (b) by the correction for longitude — *plus* 4 minutes per degree *East*, and *minus* ditto *West*, of the time Meridian.

   Example: At SIWA (Long. 25° 30′ E) on Feb. 20, watch must be retarded 14 min. for Equation of Time, and a further 18 min. for Longitude west of standard time meridian (Long. 30°). Total watch alteration 32 min.

II. Setting.   When 180° on side scale is under the pointer, the compass is correctly set for solar noon.   The shadow of the needle then gives vehicle's true bearing.   In morning, sun is to the east of south, so compass ring must be correspondingly rotated to the left.   Similarly rotate it to right in after-noon, so that red (red for sunset) scale is under pointer.   The setting of the compass ring side scale at any time is the sun's azimuth at that time, and this is given in the tables.   The setting is to be made at the **beginning** of each period and is correct for the middle of the period.   Errors at beginning and end of period cancel one another.

   The azimuths given are the means for the calendar periods heading each column.   For greater accuracy, interpolate between them.   E.g., at 9-0 a.m. on May 17 the best figure would be 96°

III. Latitude.   The sun's azimuth at any given time is less for lower latitudes than 30° and greater for higher latitudes. The variation **per degree of Lat.** is given by the small figures in each column.

TO USE.   Read vehicle's true course direct from position of shadow on top scale.   To set a fixed course, turn central disc till arrow marks required bearing.

271/2/G.H.Q.P./500/10-41.

Bagnold sun compass instructions. (Churchill Archives Centre, Ralph Bagnold, BGND)

leakage of air into the water system. Bagnold testified that "it has been common practice to run distances of 4,000 to 6,000 miles across-country in the hot weather without losing more than two pints of water."[4]

A seemingly very simple idea of immense value was to equip each vehicle with a pair of portable steel rails that would help the vehicle out of soft sand, plus two rolled-up carpets of canvas and bamboo that filled the same function. These rails and carpets, located in front of the rear wheels of a truck stuck in the soft sand, was a pretty sure way to save even the heaviest vehicles. The mats were painted white and red inside, and could be rolled out and serve as identification for aircraft.

Steel rails later became standard equipment on British wheeled vehicles in the desert. But it was the coiled sand mats on top of the front fenders that gave LRDG vehicles their special appearance.

The sun compass became another simple but crucial patrol gadget. Safe navigation had long been a problem in trackless, unknown desert. This was mainly because a magnetic compass was unreliable in a car, especially a moving one. The magnetism of shifting loads, changing gear levers and different engine speeds greatly disturb a magnetic compass. In 1928 Bagnold had modified and improved a sun compass, from which the bearing could be read accurately and quickly even when the vehicle jolted forward over uneven surfaces.[5] Simply put, it acted as a sundial with a thick needle that cast its shadow on the graduations of a circular table. It was reliable where an ordinary magnetic compass fell short. The navigator could do a reading of the bearing regardless of course changes the driver made to avoid obstacles (except on very cloudy days, when a magnetic compass outside the vehicle had to be used). Provided that the navigator also kept track of the mileometer (odometer), he could figure out the new position, at least roughly.

However, the British Army for many years did not embrace the new sun compass, even though it had been developed by one of its own officers. It was the Egyptian Army which first realized the benefits of Bagnold's design.[6] There it was made standard equipment in cars for desert use. Luckily, when Bagnold was starting up his unit, the Egyptians had just received a new shipment from the compass manufacturer in London, Watts & Co. Ralph Bagnold was thus able to borrow some of his inventions from the Egyptians, and a sun compass could eventually be mounted on each LRDG vehicle.[7]

But equally important was to be able to determine exactly where you were at the end of the day, in a landscape that not only lacked roads but often lacked any form of landmark. At the end of each day's operations each patrol thus needed a theodolite, an instrument that determines your exact position using the stars. Well, the British Army at first was able to supply the new unit with only a single theodolite! A second one was borrowed from Bagnold's old friend George Murray, director of the Egyptian Desert Examination Bureau and Pat Clayton's former boss. A third theodolite was later located in Nairobi, Kenya and flown up to Cairo.

Murray also provided support for the future LRDG by printing maps of inner Libya with the same scale as the Egyptian maps had, 1:500,000. Although these maps were largely blank - many areas were still unexplored - these sheets were nevertheless crucial for plotting courses and to record information about the terrain during missions. Since the available Italian mapping was both incomplete and often inaccurate, the patrols' geographical data was not only of great value for the British during desert battles that would later take place, it also became the foundation for several postwar maps.

4   CAC: Ralph Bagnold, BGND C 9: 'NOTES ON LONG RANGE DESERT PATROLS' dated January 1941.
5   Kennedy Shaw, p. 15.
6   Lloyd Owen, p. 16
7   Kennedy Shaw, p. 17.

The British Army had still to develop a case or box for its troops to bring along the large number of maps that were needed for long range missions. This usually meant that maps were simply rolled together and hardly protected. Each mission required a huge amount of maps and it is easy to imagine the space that hundreds of rolls of paper occupied. Well, during Bagnold's hobby desert expeditions there was even less space, and Bagnold therefore constructed plywood portfolios in which the maps were stored flat. Now he solved the problem with the same design.

All the desert travel ideas that Bagnold had introduced and tested during his expeditions years before the war could now be put into service without regard to cost. Wavell's short letter worked as an Open Sesame. When the order was handed over, the face of the recipient faded. The man would almost always deliver what had just been requested.

Regarding the first guns of the unit, the intention with the new desert patrols was primarily to conduct reconnaissance far behind enemy lines. The chosen vehicles not only lacked armour protection, they were also very open. But the patrol men could still protect themselves by cunning tactics, camouflage techniques and a liberal use of machine guns, when needed. With good tactics the crude bomber aircraft of the time were no major threat.[8] However, enemy attack aircraft could easily destroy the patrol vehicles. Unless they managed to shoot back with their machine guns or heavier guns.

Swedish anti-tank guns

General Wavell's wonderful blank cheque to Ralph Bagnold ought to have meant that he could get any weapons he desired. But in 1940 there were still limitations. There were at the time few modern machine guns to be found in Egypt. The limited availability of modern ones meant that in the initial stages one would have to do with some less than ideal types, like Lewis machine guns from the First World War and various aircraft machine guns no longer desired by the RAF.

Some LRDG vehicle crews received Swedish Bofors 37-millimeter anti-tank guns – a weapon used by a dozen armies during the Second World War. These guns enabled the patrols both to defend themselves against armoured vehicles and get that extra punch needed against Italian forts. The Bofors guns were mounted on a vertical pivot made of a discarded front wheel spindle and a ball bearing that bolted firmly to the chassis. One vehicle in each patrol got a Swedish gun.[9]

Some patrolmen had the bad fortune of getting a so-called Boys anti-tank rifle, effective only against light tanks and therefore no real help when encountering modern Panzers. It was also very long, cumbersome and the recoil was painful.

Patrols for extreme missions

During its first four months the original set of the Long Range Desert Group went by the name of Long Range Patrol Unit. But in order not to complicate things too much this book will skip that name phase.

The initial purpose of the LRDG was summed up by Bagnold with these words:

a. For reconnaissance, military, geographical and political. For propaganda among tribes and populations in distant parts of enemy territory.

---

8   CAC: Ralph Bagnold, BGND C 13 (vol II): 'THE WORK OF THE LONG RANGE DESERT GROUP' dated 12 February 1941.

9   In Sweden this gun was even mounted as the main weapon in tanks.

From the tidy looks these patrolmen in their Ford 01 V8 15-cwt have not been out that long in the desert. Note the Lewis machine gun behind the driver, pointing upwards. Also of note is the flimsy can that is connected to the engine – to save precious water. (Churchill Archives Centre, Ralph Bagnold, BGND, C12, Vol I, ID: DL 25-143A)

An early LRDG patrol consisting of two Ford 01 V8 15-cwt in the foreground and several Chevrolet WBs in the background, and more vehicles farther away. Probably taken in the Fezzan region in 1941. (Churchill Archives Centre, Ralph Bagnold, BGND, C12, Vol I, ID: DL 25-149)

Command cars

The Ford 01 commercial pickups initially used as command cars proved to be too weak for off-road driving. Replacements were received in early 1941, Ford 01V8. These worked better in the terrain but their V8 engines could not cope with the sand and thus they also had to be replaced. First with a single Ford F40 8-cwt, that was named "Te Rangi III/ Stinker". Then with Chevrolets model 1311, a smaller version of the 1533 with slightly lower ground clearance. The Chevrolet 1311 was used by all patrol officers until the final command vehicle type arrived: the Willys Jeep MB. The first specimens of this highly appreciated vehicle were SAS Jeeps that had been abandoned in the desert, salvaged by the LRDG and brought home in triumph. Thanks to skillful LRDG mechanics they could rejoin, but not the SAS. With the Jeep LRDG finally got a smaller vehicle in tune with the harsh desert environment.[10]

Heavy section vehicles

In the summer of 1940 Ralph Bagnold purchased four 6-ton Marmon Herrington heavy trucks from a mining company. They were replaced in 1941 with four 10-ton 6x4 White trucks that were superseded by four Mack MR9s, later joined by twenty Ford F60 trucks.[11] Captured Italian Lancia trucks were also put to good use, though not without some difficulty because they were diesel powered, unlike the other LRDG vehicles.

The last version of the LRDG Heavy section was divided into an anterior detachment of twenty Ford F60 CMP and a rear detachment consisting of ten Mack NR9.

Special vehicles

Each patrol had one or more vehicles with radios to maintain contact with LRDG headquarters. On the early patrol vehicles there were radios of type no. 11 mounted in a space inside the vehicle body behind the sand rails, meaning that the latter had to be removed before using the radio. Chevrolet 1533 1942 had its radio equipment in a special space not blocked by anything.

LRDG medical officer Captain Dick "Doc" Lawson had a field ambulance, a tarp covered Chevrolet 15-cwt with a special wooden body, built by some soldiers who probably had never had anything to do with car design.

All patrols also had a vehicle with a small refrigerator - in order to store serum and other sensitive medications. The same car had stretchers on the sides of the truck bed.

The LRDG also got some captured Fiat SPA AS.37, impressive-looking Italian desert trucks from the Italian *Sahariane*-companies. But they did not meet LRDG standards, despite the grotesquely large desert wheels. However, they were fine for LRDG driver training.

---

10   Jenner & List, p. 10.
11   Moreman, p. 28.

A Swedish Bofors 37mm anti-tank gun mounted on an LRDG Ford F30 in Cairo on 5 October 1941, being inspected by General Claude "The Auk" Auchinleck. The troops are wearing LRDG slip-on shoulder titles. (Alexander Turnbull Library, Wellington, N.Z. bildnr DA-06818)

Overview photo probably taken shortly before or after the previous photograph. (Churchill Archives Centre, Ralph Bagnold, BGND, C12, Vol I, ID: DL 5-52)

b.   To cause the enemy to expend fuel, vehicles and aircraft in protecting both his isolated desert posts and their supply columns against attack.[12]

The early LRDG mission concept was as follows: a mission required three patrols, each patrol consisting of two officers and 28 other ranks.

All patrolmen had to be carefully chosen volunteers. For missions so far behind enemy lines the teams had to be nothing less than perfect.

Each patrol would travel in 10 trucks plus a lighter vehicle for the patrol commander. Each patrol had to be self-sufficient with fuel, water, food rations, spare parts and ammunition. They had their own radio and could navigate and operate completely on their own for at least two weeks. During that time they should be able to travel at least 2,400 kilometres (each patrol had to carry with it fuel for at least 1,500 miles i.e. 2,400 kilometres), bearing in mind that in the desert, the terrain (rocks), often makes it impossible to drive straight.[13] Dunes have to be crossed from the right direction, causing major detours. The distance might be even longer because of the necessity to find and use provision depots laid out in advance. Such depots could not contain anything but the most insensitive, long-keeping provisions. How was it then with the meals during the sometimes months-long missions?

One of the biggest challenges for remote patrols was maintaining the men's health. They would for long periods be exposed to desiccating heat peaks during the day and with the dark immense temperature drops. Actually, it can be freezing cold in the desert!

The availability of water was severely limited. Bagnold's and his friends' experiences from before the war had shown that some physical and mental problems in the desert were directly caused by the ordinary, one-sided army diet. In particular, the lack of vegetables and other fresh foods had serious, sometimes even fatal, effects. Special food was simply a necessity or: special forces need special food.

Before the war, in the prestigious *Geographical Journal*, Bagnold had presented a more suitable diet for adventure expeditions. Again, the LRDG would benefit from Bagnold's hobby. Strangely, it seems as if Bagnold realized the military value of his hobby only after the Second World War broke out.

Receiving Bagnold's shopping list the department within the War Office (Ministry of Defence) that regulated the army diet at first refused to comply. But, brandishing Wavell's letter Bagnold got what he wanted. His patrols would receive a menu that in several ways exceeded any other British Army unit's level. Daily shots of rum were included, a practice normally restricted to the Royal Navy. Well, considering the seas of sand and naval navigation that were integral to LRDG life, some navy privileges may have been warranted.

It was not only the luxury rations that made grumpy old quartermasters raise their eyebrows when Bagnold put forward his most unusual requirements. Because patrols had to navigate after the stars over the often featureless desert, air force calendars were vital. Moreover, army boots were unsuitable for the desert, they would quickly fill with sand. So, Bagnold ordered *chaplis*, simple sandals carried by the Indian border troops. To get the best possible protection from wind, sun and sand, he chose Palestinian shawls. However, suddenly buying hundreds of Palestinian shawls in Cairo shops would raise unwelcome attention and threaten secrecy. Hence, a transfer of shawls from the Transjordan Frontier Force, many miles from curious Cairo eyes, was arranged. The shawls became popular among many patrolmen, but at times also these men preferred wearing woolen

---

12   CAC, Ralph Bagnold, BGND C 9: 'Notes of Long Range Desert Patrols' dated January 1941.
13   CAC: Ralph Bagnold, BGND C 9: 'NOTES ON LONG RANGE DESERT PATROLS' dated January 1941.

Desert food

Because of their unusually long and arduous missions, the men of the LRDG were provided with a complex and rich diet that included both Royal Navy lemon concentrate against scurvy, and rum for well-being. The aim was to let patrolmen receive the following daily (the original ounces have been converted):

bacon, tinned 70 g, bread 454 g, biscuits 340 g, cheese 43 g, chocolate 57 g, curry powder 23 g, fruit, dried 57 g, fruit, tinned 113g, herrings 43 g, jam/marmalade/golden syrup 43 g, 1 lime juice bottle, margarine 43 g meat, preserved 170 g, pickles 28 g chutney 8 g, meatloaf/ham 35 g, meat and vegetable ration 57 g, milk, tinned 57 g, mustard 3 g, oatmeal or flour 57 g, onion 57 g, pepper 8 g, potatoes, tinned 85 g, salt 21 g, salmon, tinned 28 g, sardines 28 g, sausages 28 g, sugar 100 g, tea 21 g, vegetables, tinned 113 g, ascorbic tabs, marmite 3 g, rum 28 g, tobacco or cigarettes 57 g per week, matches 2 boxes per week[14]

This was just a hint to the quartermaster when he packed the day's food in a wooden box of the same type used for two 4-gallon "flimsies" - a flimsy being a larger storage box within the British Army, made of sheet metal. In addition, the patrol would have an empty box, for opened canned food, spices etc. The quartermaster tried to choose so that the diet would be as varied as possible.

Each box contained one day's rations for 32 men, i.e. a complete patrol. That is, the box contained everything except biscuits, as army biscuits had their own tin cans. In addition, each vehicle was provided with three days of reserve provisions. Finally, each man had a one-day "iron ration" for very dire straits.

At the end of each day the patrol's second in command checked the food supply. Together with the water and petrol levels, the amount of food indicated the patrol's number of remaining operational days.[15]

(knitted) caps or black (!) berets from the Royal Armoured Corps. LRDG Association secretary Jim Patch wrote this about unit headwear in a letter to one of the authors:

The black beret was correct for desert wear [but] in the desert, we would wear almost anything on our heads [...]. Most common were either the Arab head-dress or the wollen "cap comforter" but many men wore the head-gear of their parent unit – anything from the New Zealand wide brimmed hat to the peaked cap of the Guards' Brigade.[16]

Who except Ralph Bagnold could have initiated and kick-started this most unorthodox new unit? Some people knew most things about the army and how it worked, a few had deep knowledge of the desert. Very, very few were a combination. And what's more, no one except Bagnold fully realized

14   Kennedy Shaw, p. 248.
15   CAC: Ralph Bagnold, BGND C 13 (vol II): 'Sheet 8: Long Range Desert Group: TRAINING NOTES: RATIONS, MESSING, WATER ETC' undated.
16   Letter from Jim Patch to Lars Gyllenhaal dated 10 September 1986, in the LRDG collection of Gyllenhaal.

what was needed for the upcoming missions, and at the same time had the mandate to gather all that was needed. It was typical Bagnold to early on acquire a huge amount of trouser clamps, as it was the only thing that worked to keep charts in place on map boards. Or to get kerosene-powered refrigerators, so that the medics could transport vaccine and serum in the scorching heat. Or replace army boots with sandals. But enough about trucks and gear. Are not the men who used the stuff more important? A magic letter was great for getting special gadgets, but was less effective for finding the right people.

Ralph knew enough about the British Army to refrain from seeking volunteers among the regular British troops. He was a realist. In the early days there was simply no time for a selection process, meaning no time to identify and get rid of men not fit for the tasks ahead. From day one, honest, responsible men were needed, with an initiative that regular soldiers often lack. In addition to being able to fight well, they had to be highly proficient in at least one desirable skill. Patrols many, many miles out in the desert needed truly gifted car mechanics, navigators and radio operators – and all of them had to be experienced drivers. Long periods in remote and hostile areas demanded both physical and mental forces. Everyone had to really enjoy being outdoors, and stand terrible heat. Finally, every patrolman had to be devoted both to their specialties and to the mission itself.[17]

The right volunteers

The challenge, therefore, was not finding enough volunteers. The real difficulty was to immediately find the right kind of volunteers. And this was not on General Wavell's level, but further down. More specifically, on the level of General Henry Maitland Wilson, commonly called Jumbo. He was the commander specifically of the troops in Egypt. He suggested that Ralph should try to find suitable men in the newly arrived division from New Zealand. Even though New Zealanders are generally not so fond of pommies, as they call the British, it was New Zealanders that would fit the bill best. They were often farmers or had other professions that demanded independence and initiative. Many were experienced drivers and would really take good care of their vehicles. Such an unusual attitude within the army was not only a plus in the desert, it could be crucial for the effectiveness of a unit.[18]

In addition, many of the New Zealanders were mostly sitting around, because hostile submarines had sunk a large part of their weapons and equipment.

The New Zealand commander in Africa was Major General Bernard Freyberg. A living legend. This imposing figure, with the nickname Tiny, was initially not at all helpful. Freyberg was determined to keep everyone in his division and in this aim he had the full support from his government. The troops from New Zealand and Australia participated in the Second World War on the condition that their own governments retained a great deal of control over them. Churchill could simply not use them as he wanted, but had to make inquiries.

Freyberg was particularly opposed to Bagnold depriving him of some of his best officers. But again, Ralph Bagnold got as he wanted. Freyberg was an old fan of Percy Hobart, Bagnold's friend and former boss, and that proved to be crucial.

The opportunity to volunteer for a secret and dangerous mission – meaning the LRDG, but not spelt out – immediately attracted more than a thousand men from New Zealand. However, Bagnold could borrow the New Zealanders from their government only for six months. They would

17   CAC: Ralph Bagnold, BGND C 9: 'NOTES ON LONG RANGE DESERT PATROLS' dated January 1941.
18   CAC: Ralph Bagnold, BGND C 13 (vol II): 'THE WORK OF THE LONG RANGE DESERT GROUP' dated 12 February 1941.

then return to service in the New Zealand division. Freyberg also chose two officers, Captain Bruce Ballantyne and First Lieutenant Donald Steele, and instructed them to create their own patrols from the many men who had volunteered. Interestingly, General Freyberg's own son became one of the chosen.[19]

Now, you might wonder, why no Australian soldiers? They had about the same characteristics and style. But in Australia Bagnold met some very stiff opposition. Australia's General Blamey said no. It was an absolute no.[20] Luckily, there were plenty of good New Zealanders.

When vehicles, weapons, special equipment and personnel were in place and recruited, the unit could start training together. A small but utterly realistic "exercise patrol" set off against the Italians in Libya, actually carrying a camel on board one of the trucks. With the help of the camel, one could get close to an Italian garrison without arousing any attention. This final exercise went well and demonstrated that the unit was mature for full-scale operations.

Special weapons

A special characteristic of the LRDG, in addition to having fast and desert-modified vehicles, was the fact that they had an unusual amount of guns of different kinds. There was also an urge to improve the LRDG arsenal, and therefore they were keen to use also unusual and captured weapons. During LRDG's lifetime, many weapons were used, here are just a few of them:

Vickers .50 Heavy Machine Gun, originally designed for tanks. Someone managed to "borrow" some of these from some poor tankers.

Browning .303, a gun normally found only in RAF (Royal Air Force) aircraft. These weapons the patrolmen picked up from downed aircraft. These Brownings had an electric firing system, but this was modified (simplified) by the LRDG's skilled weapon technicians. Eventually, some Browning .50 were added, most likely also from the RAF.

Breda M37, an Italian 8 millimeter machine gun, which, unlike many other Italian weapons, was really good. LRDG captured a lot of them and gladly used them.

The number of mortars was unusual; in some patrols each vehicle was equipped with a miniature mortar, designated OML 2 Inch Mortar (approximately 51 millimeters).

The personal weapon was usually a standard issue Lee-Enfield rifle, but some had the sniper version or a grenade launcher attached. Like the commandos, they also had some classic American weapons, like Thompson submachine guns, i.e. Tommy Guns. Some had captured Italian Beretta M38 submachine guns.

Captured German and Italian pistols were common among patrolmen, the most popular one was probably the Beretta M34.[21]

---

19   Lloyd Owen, p. 15; Mortimer (2015:1), p. 26.
20   *Special Forces in the Desert War 1940-43*, p. 15.
21   Jenner & List, p. 10; Moreman, p. 28; *Special Forces in the Desert War 1940-43*, p. 18.

3

Operation No. 1

Within the six weeks requested by General Wavell, Bagnold had created the first three LRDG patrols.[1] Two depots had also been established, one at the little oasis of Ain Dalla near the planned entry point into the Great Sand Sea, the other at the northern oasis town of Siwa.

In September 1940, the first LRDG patrols were very keen indeed to set off on the first real mission. But, just how big and demanding was the desert that the new unit was about to challenge? The Libyan desert, which, in spite of its name, also covers a very large part of Egypt, is larger than Egypt. It has two natural boundaries - in the north the Mediterranean and to the east the Nile. In addition it has two artificial borders, with Sudan and Chad in the south and with Tunisia to the west. The northern half consists mainly of limestone, the southern half of sandstone.[2]

Above the generally quite flat terrain there is a major plateau called Gilf Kebir. In addition, there are the mountains of Gebel Soda and Harug el Aswad plus many smaller rock formations.

Vast areas are covered by "sand seas": the Great Sand Sea, Calanshio, Rebiana and Murzuk. The Great Sand Sea is about the same size as Ireland and all of the sand seas were in 1939 considered impossible to cross by car.[3]

There is only enough rainfall every year to make a strip along the coast of North Africa green. This strip could at the time be forty kilometres deep in Libyan Cyrenaica, where it is called Gebel Akhdar. But it was only between one and three kilometres deep at Egyptian El Alamein. Over the rest of the desert there is almost no precipitation, except during those very rare rainstorms.[4] When they occur, you had better not have your camp in any of the *wadis*, the Arabic/Hebrew word referring to a valley or a dry riverbed. Because the *wadis* will fast turn into rivers that easily can push away a truck.

Here and there are a number of oases with artesian water, springs that rise from large underground lakes. The quality of the water, vegetation and settlements differs - from rugged and miserable places like Zella and Tazerbo with disgusting water and rough huts, to paradise like places like Dakhla and Siwa Oasis, with an abundance of dates, clear swimming pools and beautiful old buildings.

There are dug wells also outside the oases. Such a *bir* can seem completely dehydrated at first sight, but can contain water 12-15 meters further down.

The sun shines on most days and during high summer makes metal sizzling hot. During winter nights you can freeze to death. In the summertime 50 degrees Celsius in the middle of the day is not uncommon. Temperatures up to 60 degrees may occur with strong winds. They increase the heat in much the same way wind affects the cold.

---

1   CAC: Ralph Bagnold, BGND C 9: 'NOTES ON LONG RANGE DESERT PATROLS' dated January 1941.
2   Bagnold (2010), p. 15.
3   CAC: Ralph Bagnold, BGND C 13 (vol II): 'THE WORK OF THE LONG RANGE DESERT GROUP' dated 12 February 1941.
4   Ibid.

Then there is the desert silence and beauty. Bill Kennedy Shaw described these aspects with the following words in his war memoirs:

It was quiet, at times so silent that you found yourself listening for something to hear. And it was beautiful too, not at midday when the hills look flat and lifeless, but in the early morning or late evening when they throw cool, dark shadows and the low sun makes you marvel at the splendid symmetry of the yellow dunes. A psychologist would say, perhaps, that to take pleasure in deserts is a form of escapism, a surrender to the same impulses which made hermits of the early Christians, a refusal to face the unpleasant realities of modern life. He may be right; there are a lot of things in this life worth escaping from, even if only for half an hour at the end of the day´s run of an LRDG patrol.[5]

Mussolini starts the party

The news of Benito Mussolini's declaration of war on 10 June 1940 radically changed the mood in Cairo. But after the declaration, the Italian side had gone strangely silent and seemingly passive. General Wavell, on the other hand, did not sit still. He ordered the 7th Armoured Division, the Desert Rats, to blow up 45 openings in the border fence that Italy´s Marshal Balbo had put up in the 1930s to prevent the Senussi from moving across the Libyan-Egyptian border line. The Senussi was a political and religious Muslim order that Italy had been fighting since the First World War.

The holes that the Desert Rats blew open were numbered, so that the patrols could better report if there were any Italian movements. Through the openings, British reconnaissance patrols could also get out and find out more about the enemy's dispositions. Soon the British knew nearly everything about what the Italian defense system looked like, where the weak points were, their numbers and especially how many Italian tanks there were in the region.

The Italian Army under Marshal Graziani had established a long line of forts on its side of the desert border, and their troops rarely ventured far from them. It was outdated thinking. But then the Italians actually began to move. Shortly before 4 September 1940 the British headquarters understood that the enemy prepared some type of offensive operation in the desert, from 'Uweinat. Perhaps Mussolini wanted to strike against Sudan?

The Italian headquarters had radio connections with the remote oases and had aircraft based in Jalo and Kufra and was able to send patrols to 'Uweinat. Information about British forces probably leaked from the Egyptian oases, particularly from Siwa. Far from all Egyptians were positive to the British. That was not a new attitude, but had until recently been of little consequence.

On 4 September, LRDG finally received the first mission order. Aside from training the patrols in working together and collecting data about the terrain on their journey, three clear tasks were given:

- Establish dumps of petrol, food and water along the border with Libya.
- Perform long distance reconnaissance north and south of the Kufra Oasis.
- Raid and destroy any enemy dumps and other enemy installations at 'Uweinat.[6]

The mission was organized as follows: the mission commander and his staff would travel in a light 15-cwt Ford Pilot, three patrols - each with two officers and 25 men - would travel in 10 Chevrolet 30-cwt trucks, all equipped and ready for operating independently during 20 days and 2,400 kilometres. Actually, no motorized unit had ever been given the task of operating without support so far away in the desert.

5   Kennedy Shaw, p. 31.
6   *Special Forces in the Desert War 1940-43*, pp. 19-20.

The heaviest weapon that each patrol would bring along was a Bofors 37mm cannon. In addition, each patrol would be armed with four Boys anti-tank guns, 10 Lewis machine guns, plus personal weapons.

In the morning of 5 September at 09.00, W Patrol set off under the command of Captain Edward "Teddy" Mitford (yes, a relative of the Nazi Mitford sisters). Their first major objective was Ain Dalla, at the outskirts of the Great Sand Sea. Mitford's W Patrol would be accompanied by LRDG commander Ralph Bagnold and his intelligence officer, Bill Kennedy Shaw.

R Patrol started half an hour later, at 09.30, and T Patrol after another half an hour.

The first destination of the three patrols was common: the oasis of Siwa. But they would not travel to Siwa together. There were already plenty of ears and eyes in Cairo that worked for Mussolini and Hitler. A large number of specially modified vehicles heading out into the desert could raise unwelcome attention.

The maintenance people had a particularly vital role in an extreme desert unit like the LRDG. Should not Lieutenant Holliman and his maintenance team succeed in setting up two depots in exactly the right places, the patrols would not only fail, their men would most probably die. The maintenance group's vehicles were at this time mainly two heavy six wheeled Marmon-Herringtons. In order to avoid unnecessary wear, these trucks were transported by rail to Assuan in southern Egypt and then driven to El Kharg.[7] This was the place from which petrol and water was transported to the depots at Bir Misaha and the southern end of the Gilf Kebir mountain plateau. Four truck loads for each dump. The main idea with these was that the action radius of patrols was significantly increased by filling up from these depots before moving on deeper into the desert.

Secrets of long range

African deserts, Greenland and Antarctica. These places have something in common – a need for depots. In order to carry out long range journeys in these areas, one must have access to depots with fuels, food, and in the desert also water. Therefore, the first part of the LRDG's first operation was to set up a depot at Big Cairn in September 1940.[8] This depot was the prerequisite for further missions into Northern Libya.

The first operational patrols filled up from dumps between 480 and 800 kilometres from their starting points. Thus, they were able to carry out assignments 1,600 to 1,900 further away than possible with only their own supplies of petrol, water and food. The locations of the depots of course changed with the tide of war. The depots were laid out using heavy trucks.

The LRDG's own aircraft were also dependent on being able to refuel on the simple airfields established by the Gilf Kebir and Big Cairn. These are places where lots of Second World War British petrol cans still remain, more than seventy years later.

But not only planned operations and aircraft require depots. While moving supplies from Mersa Matruh to Siwa, the heavy section under First Lieutenant Arnold established depots of food, water, shoes, etc. in a line from Jarabub to Bir Etla, a distance of 320 kilometres. These depots were intended primarily for patrolmen who had experienced some disaster, to help them survive while they were heading back to civilization. They were also vital for aircraft crews and prisoners of war, who were evading through the desert back to the British lines.

---

7   *Special Forces in the Desert War 1940-43*, p. 20.
8   Kennedy Shaw, p. 41.

What did the individual patrolman have with him on a long range patrol? Everyone: officers, NCOs and other ranks, was given the same type of sleeping mat and blanket. Aside from the uniform items being worn on the body all men would also have greatcoats and some personal belongings packed in a small canvas bag.[9]

The ammunition quota during a standard patrol was 200 rounds per rifle, 18 rounds per pistol, 20 filled magazines per machine gun plus an emergency ammo box. Every Bofors gun would have 120 rounds, Boys anti-tank guns would have a 100.

Each patrol had its own route and a detailed plan to execute all given tasks. An accurately set up system of depots – that was the secret that enabled the LRDG already during its first operation to travel enormous stretches without support other than that from the depots.

"Roderick Berlin"

It was of utmost importance that as little information as possible was broadcast by radio and thus risk being picked up by the enemy. Fixed transmission times gave the enemy the opportunity to locate positions and glean British frequencies and signals. Therefore, long and continuous broadcasts had to be avoided and both transmission times and frequencies had to be changed all the time. A patrol that could not transmit quickly and accurately was almost a useless patrol.[10] Every geographical name that might have to be mentioned in a message was thus given a new name before the first operation (of course, these names were then changed before new assignments). Just a few examples: Cairo = Pool, Dalla = Berlin, the Dalla-depot = Rome and Siwa = Chatham. Also, some regular nouns and actions were given code names. For example, meeting point = Arnold, return to = Humprey, attacked by aircraft = Jones, we are moving towards = Roderick. Now you can figure out the meaning of "Roderick Berlin".

The W Patrol's journey between Cairo and the springs at Ain Dalla was completed in two days and was unproblematic. In the morning of 7 September the patrol was on its way again, and the first major dunes began to appear about 30 kilometres after the springs. The dune belt here is approximately 260 kilometres wide, yet this is the narrowest point in the whole of the Great Sand Sea. Ralph Bagnold´s and Pat Clayton´s hobby expeditions before the war had shown that this was the only place south of Siwa that was possible for passage westwards by motor vehicle.

Even aside from the fact that the "waves" were 40-50 meters high, the Great Sand Sea had its name for a good reason for the name, it felt like an ocean. Everyone feels tiny in it. Quite a few of the patrolmen who had not previously been with Bagnold in the desert in this situation probably doubted that they would be able to get through with all the trucks loaded to the limit. Certainly, the suspension had been reinforced with extra springs, but so far they had mostly been driving on solid ground. Now they would have to drive through deep sand, so fine you sank deeply into it as you walked.

A demonstration was required.

With the entire W Patrol standing on a slope as observers and pupils, Ralph Bagnold sat behind the wheel on one of the trucks and steered full throttle against the sand barrier in front of him.[11]

A failure now would not only endanger this first operation.

The man sitting beside Bagnold was clinging to his seat when the sand rose up steeply and the car was still doing some 80 kilometres per hour. The spectators could see the nose lift and the wheels

---

9   CAC: Ralph Bagnold, BGND C 9: 'NOTES ON LONG RANGE DESERT PATROLS' dated January 1941.
10   Jenner & List, p. 16.
11   Kennedy Shaw, p. 38.

almost lift off from the ground, the treacherous sand. But this driving strangely enough brought the heavily laden truck right up to the top, where Bagnold made a smooth turn and stopped.

The rejoicing of the spectators was a fine reward. Had anyone doubted Ralph Bagnold's desert skills, this doubt was now gone.

It's the first 40 meters that count, if you can handle them without faltering the rest will be OK as long as you know where to go when you reach the top. The air pressure is also important – it must be varied to suit the type of ground surface. Over soft sand it is necessary to reduce the pressure between the tread and the ground to a minimum. This is done by deflating the tyre and thus increasing the area of the tread in contact with the ground.[12]

Shortly afterwards, Bill Kennedy Shaw too had to demonstrate his driving skills, and was able to recall lessons learnt.[13] But when one of the regular drivers then tried to drive, he got stuck.

Bagnold and Kennedy Shaw had shown the art of crossing a dune, but just watching them did not equal learning. The drivers made all the mistakes that could be made. Nerves of steel and a cool head are required to drive full speed against a sand barrier, and most, at first, lacked those characteristics. But soon the patrolmen learnt.

Do not drive into other tracks.

No wild gear changing going uphill in the slope.

Lastly, attempts to step on it when losing speed (because you had been slow in the start) invariably meant getting stuck. Within an hour all the vehicles, except the two steered by the desert veterans, were sitting on the slope. Swearing and sweating, the men were digging for hours to be able to move on. Somewhat wiser.

It took W Patrol and Bagnold's staff car two days of hard work to reach Big Cairn at the western end of the Great Sand Sea. Here, Pat Clayton in 1932 had built a cairn, only one and a half meter high. But even such a modest height is eye-catching in the desert, noticed from far away.[14] Here the patrol deposited all reserves of water and petrol. While Bagnold personally started plotting for a landing ground, Captain Mitford took W Patrol back to Ain Dalla to pick up more petrol. It was important to fill the Big Cairn fuel dump properly for future trips.

It was clear that the drivers had learnt something from Bagnold's dune driving demonstration: when it was time to move on only two vehicles got stuck.

A month earlier Bill Kennedy Shaw had put up a big depot at Ain Dalla using the two six-wheel Marmon-Herrington trucks. For him it was familiar terrain, because he had been there as a civilian in 1930, part of a group travelling in three A-Fords. In the hard terrain he could actually distinguish their track from 1930. It was really only here, in a belt between 15 and 30 kilometers wide, that it was possible to pass the Great Sand Sea. From the Gilf Kebir or Siwa it was impossible. Many, perhaps also the Italians, thought it was impossible even here. But Ralph Bagnold had firmly stated to General Wavell that it was possible. Now he was proving it.

When the Italians in a rather prudent style started their offensive on 10 September 1940, the LRDG was right beside the border of Italy's huge colony, Libya, and 500 kilometers south of the Mediterranean. After advancing about 80 kilometers, the Italian offensive stopped at Sidi Barrani, where they set up a series of fortified camps that proved to be a bit too far from each other. The British defenders largely retreated, but their fast-moving armoured reconnaissance cars could race with ease between the sparse Italian positions. The Italian generals seemed to have forgotten which century it was.

12   CAC: Ralph Bagnold, BGND C 9: 'NOTES ON LONG RANGE DESERT PATROLS' dated January 1941.
13   Kennedy Shaw, p. 37.
14   Kennedy Shaw, p. 41.

In W Patrol, it was quiet. The other two patrols arrived at a predetermined rendezvous, where an exchange of experiences was possible, which was important, especially for Bagnold. This first long trip was not least about gaining experience for future tasks. Lessons learnt were studied again and again, both in terms of men's performance and the merits and drawbacks of their vehicles and equipment.

After a few days, the patrols proceeded westwards to the Calanshio Sand Sea, not marked on Italian maps and a smaller formation than the Great Sand Sea.[15] It was actually Pat Clayton who had once "discovered" it, i.e. it had previously not been on the maps, even though Bedouins knew about it.

On 16 September, W Patrol, without unwelcome Italian attention, reached the Jalo-Kufra Road, which was more of a track.[16] It had seen a lot of traffic lately, it was easy to estimate the direction and frequency of the traffic from the tire tracks in the sand.[17]

While they were on the Libyan side of the border W Patrol was attacked, not by Italians, but by a *ghibli*, a hot wind that dropped straight on the patrol.[18] It was no true sandstorm, but the sand that the southern wind brought with it dotted the skin like needles, and it became difficult to eat. It was hot, hot, hot. Bill Kennedy Shaw, who had profound experiences from many countries, explained how everyone has their own warm winds; Egypt has its *khamseen*, Palestine its *sherqiya* and West Africa its *harmattan*. None of them, however, are close to being as hot as the *ghibli*: "You don't merely feel hot, you don't merely feel tired, you feel as if every bit of energy had left you, as if your brain was thrusting its way through the top of your head".

But the show must go on. That same day, W Patrol reached the Italian Emergency Airfield No. 4, along the Jalo-Kufra flight route, which coincides with the trail. There they destroyed the petrol pumps, the small fuel supply and the wind indicator.[19] The patrol continued to follow the track to Emergency Airfield No. 3, where about 500 litres of aviation fuel was put on fire together with a shed. Still no Italians in sight. Then the patrol reached the Marada-Tazerbo route, marked with three-meter high iron posts with roundels on top that made them visible from the air. The posts stood a kilometer apart, and between them stood empty steel drums to mark the trail when it was hard to discern. Again, car tracks were examined and they were then compared with earlier observations.

Unusually hot winds still raged. The next day, all patrols changed direction and drove towards Tazerbo, and that evening was probably the worst so far. Everyone was ill. Not even the old desert hands had experienced so much pressing heat. In addition to the high temperature, probably 45-50 degrees Celsius, a very hot wind was blowing from the south or east. A number of cases of heat stroke among men could not be avoided. When it was worst there was no alternative but to stay still in the shade and wait. One could not talk, barely even think.

Water rations

One of the most important things for the patrols to test was the allotted water ration. During their first major mission the ration was three litres a day. It was served as a half-litre in the morning, a half-litre in the lime juice at lunch for the prevention of scurvy and a litre for the evening tea. Finally, the litre for the water bottle, which could be consumed at its owner´s discretion.

---

15   Julian Thompson, *War Behind Enemy Lines* (London: Sidgwick & Jackson, 1998).
16   Kennedy Shaw, p. 42.
17   *Special Forces in the Desert War 1940-43*, p. 20.
18   The Italian word *ghibli* was picked up from Libyan Arabic.
19   *Special Forces in the Desert War 1940-43*, p. 20.

During the winter, three litres a day was quite okay, during a normal summer in the desert, almost bearable. But during a real *ghibli*, this ration felt like nothing. Still, one could survive with that amount, and there were those who were worse off. Like migratory birds. Sometimes there were plenty of them, sitting around, half dead or soon dead. It was hard to cope with the strain. When the patrols stopped for a pause or rest, the birds flew under the cars in dozens. They were sometimes even offered some water by kind patrolmen, but many birds rejected it, feeling that it was not worth the effort, as they were about to die.[20]

Water facts

In the desert it is crystal clear that water means life. Water was no private matter but always something that concerned the whole unit. To directly quote from the LRDG Training Notes:

> Rapid drinking during the heat of the day must be avoided, nearly all the water is merely thrown off again in excessive perspiration, and the water is wasted. The first cravings for water are lessened by moistening the mouth and throat. Take small sips from the water bottle. [...] On arrival at a water-hole, all water containers will be filled before washing or any [other] activity is started.[21]

The summer allotment of water was increased after some experience; the minimum amount was determined to be 1 gallon (4.54 litres) per man per day.[22] The water was transported in sealed 4-gallon metal containers, so-called flimsies, and in two-gallon containers. The latter had a screw top where the usual leather washer was replaced by a rubber one made from an old inner tube. This was done in order to prevent fouling of the water by the leather. If you missed this detail, the many desert transports made your water taste like leather. In order that the water tanks would not rust from inside, the inner surfaces were coated with high melting point paraffin wax.

The water supply was counted in gallons, not containers. When the vehicle commander counted and reported water status he always had to omit the reserve, i.e. 8 gallons and what was lying in the radiator overflow tin.

During the daily water check, the total reported water stocks divided by the number of men in the party immediately showed the numbers of days the party could continue without more water supplies.[23]

Two days later, near the empty Italian emergency airfield No. 7, the LRDG for the first time fired some shots in anger. Out of nowhere, two Italian six-ton trucks appeared. They turned out to be the bi-weekly supply convoy to the Italian base in Kufra. A single burst of British machine gun fire above the vehicles constituted the prelude, climax and final act of this battle. Immediately

20   Kennedy Shaw, p. 44.
21   CAC: Ralph Bagnold, BGND C 13 (vol II): 'Sheet 9: Long Range Desert Group: TRAINING NOTES: RATIONS, MESSING, WATER ETC' undated, p. 1.
22   CAC: Ralph Bagnold, BGND C 13 (vol II): 'Sheet 9: Long Range Desert Group: TRAINING NOTES: RATIONS, MESSING, WATER ETC' undated, p. 1.
23   CAC: Ralph Bagnold, BGND C 13 (vol II): 'Sheet 9: Long Range Desert Group: TRAINING NOTES: RATIONS, MESSING, WATER ETC' undated, p. 1.

thereafter, the first prisoners of war were welcomed by the LRDG: two civilian Italian drivers, two native assistants, one police officer, three native passengers and one goat. The war booty was slightly better. About 10,000 litres of petrol and a whole bag of official mail that together with the results of the prisoner interrogations was later handed over to headquarters in Cairo, with some satisfaction.[24] The mail turned out to contain all the enemy dispositions in the inner desert area.[25]

The Italian trucks were a valuable addition. Capturing vehicles was no unimportant thing. Germany´s desert war mastermind General Erwin Rommel was an expert at using captured vehicles, like when he took Tobruk: thousands of vehicles and millions of litres of petrol. And that was not the only time that British taxpayers helped the German Afrika Korps.

Unfortunately, the two captured Italian trucks ran on diesel, and the LRDG was petrol-driven. Some days later, when the fuel in the Italian trucks was low, they were hidden in Gilf Kebir. The eight prisoners of war from the trucks got a free ride to Cairo.

While leaving the airfield, it was noted that nearby there were excellent places for setting up ambushes. But the trip back home to Cairo passed without mishaps. During daytime W Patrol only had sporadic contact with Bagnold's staff car, but in the evenings they would meet up. The 15-cwt Ford Pilot staff car was not a vehicle suitable for unaccompanied travel in the desert. It was not as reliable a machine as the others and it could not carry enough fuel, water and rations. After many troubles it was dropped as an LRDG vehicle. Ralph Bagnold was constantly trying to learn from the lessons that reality offered.

However, reality did not always affect the thinking of the British Army. The Army's standard petrol cans deserve a special mention. Before capturing large amounts of the excellent German petrol containers, soon called jerrycans (jerry = from the slang word for Germans), the patrols were equipped only with standard issue British flimsy cans, also called flimsies. These came two and two in wooden boxes that became excellent fuel for campfires in the evenings. But it was also the only advantage against the brilliantly designed jerrycan.

The fuel losses caused by leaking flimsies were very large, almost legendary. Leaks of 25 percent were quite normal, but on very long range missions in difficult terrain they were even higher. The problem with the containers was basically the thin metal and soldered seams, which easily split during transportation. This in combination with something as predictable as the African sand and the vehicle's motion from the rough terrain resulted in nearly invisible little holes. Everywhere in Cairo and the oases, you could see these four-gallon cans in civilian use: as containers, flower pots on porches and, not least, roofing. They were practical, almost indispensable. They were tremendously useful, yes, for everything except transporting petrol in the desert.

The original German containers, *Wehrmacht-Einheitskanister*, really only had one disadvantage: they did not provide any wood for campfires.

The Americans and Brits eventually learned to copy the much better German petrol containers, but failed to initially equip them with a good spout, one that did not spill. Like the German spout.

During the first LRDG mission W Patrol met the other two patrols a few times, but what more did they do? The main task of the first mission was reconnaissance, and since only W Patrol had contact with the enemy, the others could focus on analyzing the terrain, primarily its accessibility for different types of vehicles. When T Patrol on 17 September visited an empty Italian airfield 108 kilometres southwest of Kufra the patrol resisted the urge to demolish its infrastructure because they did not want to at this time alert the attention of the Italian garrison in 'Uweinat.

---

24   Kennedy Shaw, 45; *Special Forces in the Desert War 1940-43*, p. 21.
25   CAC: Ralph Bagnold, BGND C 13 (vol II): 'THE WORK OF THE LONG RANGE DESERT GROUP' dated 12 February 1941, p. 4.

Getting a Ford 01 V8 15-cwt back in motion. Note the mix of greatcoats, one possibly of naval origin, and "Hebron" fur coats. (Churchill Archives Centre, Ralph Bagnold, BGND, C12, Vol I, ID: DL 25-156)

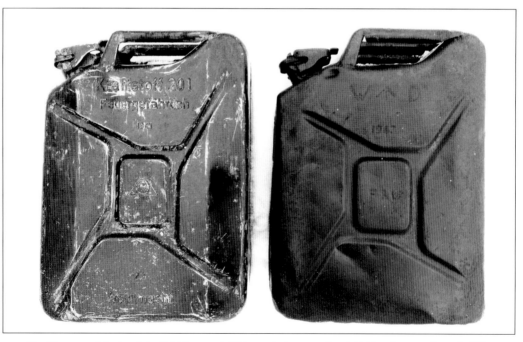

The German original and the British copy. A Wehrmacht jerrycan dated 1941 and a copy from the War Department (WD) dated 1943. (Lars Gyllenhaal)

Desert fuel

There were no petrol stations in the desert. Nor was it possible to quickly get motor oil, tires, belts and perform serious repairs. Therefore, the patrols brought along engine oil and lubricants and one of the cars was a veritable rolling workshop. All vehicles got solid maintenance every night. And, of course should always be filled up to allow maximum range in case of action. The average patrol vehicle had petrol for 2,400 kilometres, meaning that the cars consumed about 2.1 litres per 10 kilometres. By refueling in fuel dumps, the distance could be vastly increased.

Refueling during an operation was precisely recorded and compared to the mileometer to immediately detect leaks and incorrectly adjusted carburetors and other problems that could lead to increased fuel consumption. Every evening, the fuel supply was estimated as accurately as possible. Each vehicle had a name, not least because each one had its own character, best known by the driver who was responsible for it. Bagnold's commitment to mainly recruit farmers as drivers gave full dividend. These drivers had a longer engine experience than their peers from towns and truly understood the value of maintenance.

The first LRDG operation yielded vital training and good intelligence from prisoners, observations etc. But it also proved that most of the vehicles and equipment had been chosen wisely.

During the first mission the patrols drove a total of some 150,000 miles without serious mechanical errors. Yes, a truck did roll over as it traversed a dune in the Great Sand Sea, but without suffering any real damage. A connection was worn and needed to be replaced. Important feedback regarding the maps was noted. There were too many lines on them, making it difficult to add new observations made on the spot. The solution was to alter the next print run of LRDG maps.

Bagnold's somewhat strange choice of standard vehicle for the LRDG had been justified. The 30-cwt Chevrolet was a truck designed for civilian use, but now it had passed a test far harder than any other.

There were different types of patrol vehicles because there were different roles to fill. However, one of the vehicles was far more valuable than the others, the radio truck. Without it a patrol could not send its observations to HQ. Nor could it receive information about enemy movements in the area, or receive time signals. The radios plus proficiency in long range signals was at the heart of the Group´s ability to carry out their demanding operations.

The radio truck had a specially built section on the right side behind the driver that could be reached from outside, and there was the radio. Bagnold chose the army's light radio no. 11, in spite of it being standard issue. The thing is that it was able to receive and transmit at significantly longer distances than expected. The range was officially 120 kilometers, but for a short period each day it would have a much larger range according to a schedule varying with season and latitude. Although it was not perfect for the desert, not much else was available. The last available no. 11 set in the Middle East went to LRDG's third patrol, thanks to Ralph's magical letter.

For those really long range broadcasts the radio truck had two collapsible 4-meter bars. Connected with a copper wire to each other they formed a very effective radio antenna. Unfortunately, it was not always possible to mount that antenna, like when you were near the coastal road to record enemy vehicle movements.

Apart from a communication radio, the radio truck also had a good receiver, which was mainly used to receive the time signal from Greenwich. Without it, the exact position of the patrol could not be determined using the stars. Teaching this kind of navigation, creating six navigators, fell on Bill Kennedy Shaw. Unexpected assistance came from Private Dick Croucher. He had kept silent about his navigational experience from the New Zealand Merchant Navy, so as to not risk getting behind a desk instead of frontline service. Now his navigation skills came to good use, he became a teacher for future LRDG navigators.

Desert navigation

The minimum crew for an LRDG truck was three, and this was not just because at least three men were needed to get a car unstuck in the desert. The number was determined by the fact that aside from a driver and a navigator there always had to be one person onboard focusing on enemy aircraft. Navigation in the army meant that one person set a course that applied to a number of vehicles, and then held it regardless of the terrain. This meant strong wear on vehicles and the men themselves. In dunes and cliff terrain it is impossible to do it that way. Here, each car driver must decide which route choice is best. LRDG applied "dead reckoning", a method commonly used in shipping. The principle is that if you know how long, how quickly and in what direction you have moved from a certain point, you also know where you are. With the solar compass, a clock and the car's mileometer, the car's navigator constantly kept track of where the vehicle was, and the margin for a good navigator was about 3 percent in distance and 1.5 degrees in the bearing.

However, dead reckoning was not good enough for the very big distances of LRDG operations. Since errors in dead reckoning accumulate on a daily basis, it was absolutely necessary to complement the method with astronomy, by determining the exact position of the patrol with a three-star astronomical fix. For this reason each patrol vehicle carried a theodolite to determine the sun´s height, a radio that was able to receive London's time signal, and a reliable clock. The sextant option was rejected because the libelles, the small liquid containers that served as water passes, would not be able handle the shaking during the journey. Theodolites were not as sensitive. Each patrol had two navigators who, after thorough training, were promoted to NCOs with navigation as a specialty.[26]

During the patrols' absence from Cairo in September 1940, big things had happened. The British Middle East Command had previously appealed to the War Office that the LRDG should be doubled. While London was contemplating this plea the Italian Army launched its offensive against Sidi Barrani, which demonstrated the seriousness of the situation. On 29 September the War Office gave the green light for an extension. A larger LRDG headquarters would be created with its own separate radio vehicle and its own maintenance section, and under this new HQ there would be two squadrons with three patrols.

But where to find men for LRDG enlargement? In spite of everything, the New Zealand Division Commander General Freyberg now called back his men. The Division's various parts had now reached the Nile delta, and their equipment would soon be in place. Freyberg had his government behind him, but the situation after the Italian offensive was desperate. The LRDG had a key role in countering the Italians and General Wilson thus simply refused to comply with

26   CAC: Ralph Bagnold, BGND C 9: 'NOTES ON LONG RANGE DESERT PATROLS' dated January 1941, pp. 8-11.

Freyberg's demand. He decided, however, that the New Zealanders would return to their parent units as soon as trained replacements could be brought in from British and Southern Rhodesian units to the LRDG. All this would be addressed alongside the issue of expanding the unit.

The enlarged LRDG had to be led by at least 16 officers, and there were no small demands to become an LRDG officer. A candidate must, in addition to being a true volunteer, also have high IQ, be enterprising and willing to take on all tasks even if he had never come into contact with them before. Meaning a willingness to learn navigation and advanced military communications, interaction with aircraft, complicated logistics, etc. And aside from this, be mechanically talented. In practice this meant that the candidate had better have previous experience of working with vehicles in extreme environments.[27]

It was also no easy thing to become one of the about 250 NCOs and other ranks within the LRDG, even one of the 20 men who mostly stayed in the LRDG bases. There were plenty of volunteers, and it was not uncommon for interested people to ask that their rank should not count, to get in. Thus, many LRDG privates had been NCOs who had done absolutely everything possible to join.

That every patrol member had to be able to handle every LRDG weapon could hardly surprise candidates, but LRDG egalitarianism went further. Ranks existed but were completely disregarded when it came to standing guard, cleaning dishes and getting the cars unstuck. One has to understand that in the regular British Army such equality was at the time just about unthinkable.

Every LRDG private had to have a specialty, without one he simply had no place in the organization. Driver specialists had to be first class. However, even really good road drivers might experience great difficulties in rough terrain, so more driver specialists than necessary were accepted and a number of them were sent back (returned to unit, RTU). Of course, car mechanics had to also be top-notch, and preferably have desert experience of both Chevrolet and Ford trucks.[28]

In late 1940 at least 12 more navigators were needed, either already proficient, or expected to quickly learn how to make astronomical observations and determine from them the geographical position. In this case the LRDG had to look through the entire Middle East command for appropriate volunteers. It would be an advantage if more than 12 could be recruited, to allow further expansion of the LRDG.

As many as possible of the newcomers should be used to Lewis and Vickers machine guns, and enough of the new NCOs had to be able to teach the handling of these weapons.

Finally, another 37 Chevrolet trucks were needed, which were not available for purchase in the Middle East, or even could be purchased from the United States. The attempt to buy more cars from the Egyptian Army failed. But Ralph Bagnold would solve this problem too.[29]

---

27   CAC: Ralph Bagnold, BGND C 9: 'NOTES ON LONG RANGE DESERT PATROLS' dated January 1941.
28   Ibid.
29   Vanderveen, pp. 14-21.

4

'Ain Zwaya and 'Ain Dua

In early October 1940, Ralph Bagnold received the following letter:

General Headquarters,
Middle East,
Cairo.

1st October, 1940.

Dear Bagnold,

I should like you to convey to the officers and other ranks under your command my congratulations and appreciation of the successful results of the recent patrols carried out by your unit in Central Libya.

I am aware of the extreme physical difficulties which had to be overcome, particularly the intense heat.

That your operation, involving as it did 150,000 truck miles, has been brought to so successful a conclusion indicates a standard of efficiency in preparation and execution of which you, your officers and men may be justly proud.

A full report of your exploits has already been telegraphed to the War Office, and I wish you all the best of luck in your continued operations, in which you will be making an important contribution towards keeping Italian forces in back areas on the alert and adding to the anxieties and difficulties of our enemy.

Yours sincerely,
A. P. Wavell[1]

Strengthened by this encouragement, the LRDG vigorously prepared themselves for their second operation. It would start on 24 October 1940 and had three purposes. Mainly to disturb the Italians by mining the Uweinat-Kufra-Jedabia road and acquiring knowledge of the movements of the air and land forces between this road and the Egyptian border. The LRDG was also supposed to catch some prisoners, in able to obtain some detailed up-to-date information, plus bring home both of the Italian trucks previously concealed.[2]

T and R Patrols were assigned to the operation. There was a pleasant novelty, the Royal Air Force would help with the maintenance by ordering No. 216 Squadron to fly supplies to Baharia and other forward LRDG bases.

---

1   Kennedy Shaw, p. 47.
2   *Special Forces in the Desert War 1940-43*, p. 26.

T Patrol under Pat Clayton left Cairo with the main task of mining the Jalo route. But first, the Patrol headed towards Ain Dalla, crossed the Great Sand Sea and reached Big Cairn. There a landing field had been prepared and now it ought to be inaugurated. The RAF was perhaps not in the best mood, it had assigned only one Vickers Type 264 Valentia, with six men, for the support work.

Vickers Type 264 Valentia was a biplane bomber and cargo machine designed to operate in the colonies and preferably without encountering any hostile flights. The fast development of aircraft had not been kind to the Valentia, although only six years old it was already outdated. Nevertheless, the LRDG gained important insights from the first support flights. One was that with the help of airplanes, the LRDG staff could attain a deeper level of contact with the patrols while they were out on their missions, and thus better direct them when necessary. Thanks to the Valentias it was also possible to investigate how visible the traces of the patrols were from the air. If the patrol vehicles drove in the same track after each other, their traces proved to be easy to detect from the air, even from high altitude. If, on the other hand, the cars spread out it became much more difficult for hostile flights to follow the unit, especially if the drivers sometimes made an abrupt turn.

After Big Cairn, the T Patrol steered northwest, passing the newly discovered Calanshio Sand Sea, which was not found on any maps, and reached the Ajedabia-Jalo road. There, no less than six road sections were mined, and then they proceeded towards the Fascist outpost in the Aujila Oasis. Here, the Italians were completely unprepared for hostile action. A Libyan soldier in Italian service who was strolling along on the outpost's main street was simply paralyzed when T Patrol suddenly appeared and told him to hand over his weapon. Having reached the Italian fort, some rounds from the Bofors anti-tank gun sent a flock of pigeons beating upward, whereupon the garrison ran away to hide in a palm grove.[3]

From Aujila, T Patrol took a prisoner as well as two heavy Austro-Hungarian machine guns and a number of Italian Carcano rifles.[4] They spent a total of 15 days in the desert and traveled 3,450 kilometres. Later it became known that the patrol's road mining had cost the Italians at least half a dozen trucks.

When interrogated in Cairo the prisoner revealed valuable information. The Jalo garrison comprised only 50 native soldiers and two Italians, but at Giarabub there were no less than 1,500 men. In Sidi Barrani there were about 2,500 Arabic troops in Italian service, and the general perception among them was that they would be pushed in front of the Italians to function as their shields. He also said that the Italians had spread a rumor that the British killed their prisoners, and that the goal of British air bombings was to kill civilians. However, the native soldiers did not believe this because the number of killed civilians had been minimal. Furthermore, the Italians were convinced that Siwa was so strongly fortified that it was not realistic to attack the British there. Also, the prisoner claimed that an outcome of the LRDG's first operation was that Italian vehicles were not sent to Kufra other than in well-protected convoys.[5]

It was part of Bagnold's overall plan to force the enemy to guess wildly where the LRDG would appear next. They made such an impression on the Italians that they started calling them *Pattuglia Fantasma*, meaning Ghost Patrol.

A few days before T Patrol struck at Aujila, R Patrol had split up, to mine the routes around 'Uweinat and pick up those two hidden Italian trucks. There were two Italian Army positions with airfields west of the 'Uweinat mountain massif, the bases 'Ain Zwaya and 'Ain Dua. This made the 'Uweinat area an Italian stronghold and a starting point for causing trouble across the border, in

---

3   *Special Forces in the Desert War 1940-43*, p. 26.
4   The rifle name may ring a bell, it was a Carcano that later was used to assassinate US President John F. Kennedy.
5   *Special Forces in the Desert War 1940-43*, pp. 28-29.

Egypt. In fact, fears of this had been an important factor behind the establishment of the LRDG. Not only Egypt could be threatened from there, aircraft based at 'Uweinat could hit targets in Sudan and Eritrea, and in addition, spy on French Equatorial Africa. So, the LRDG would have to get a grip on the 'Uweinat area.

LRDG organization

The first version of the unit consisted of three patrols:
R (from New Zealand)
T (from New Zealand)
W (from New Zealand)

By the end of 1940 G Patrol (from the Brigade of Guards) were added.
    In June 1941, the LRDG consisted of two squadrons comprising a total of six patrols (three per squadron):
G (from the Brigade of Guards)
H (from the Brigade of Guards and Yeomanry)
Y (Yeomanry)
S (from Rhodesia)
T (from New Zealand)
R (from New Zealand)

In October 1941, the LRDG was extended to 10 patrols:
R1 (from New Zealand)
R2 (from New Zealand)
T1 (from New Zealand)
T2 (from New Zealand)
G1 (Guards)
G2 (Guards)
S1 (from Rhodesia)
S2 (from Rhodesia)
Y1 (Yeomanry)
Y2 (Yeomanry)

Aside from that the patrols at times were divided into two troops, this organization was retained until April 1943.[6]

On 24 October, Bill Kennedy Shaw and parts of R Patrol steered towards 'Ain Zwaya to there mine the trail to Kufra and find something more to disturb the sleep of Italian commanders. The raiders were in luck. On the western runway, the patrol found and destroyed a Savoia Marchetti SM.79 *Sparviero*, meaning Sparrowhawk but often called "the damn hunchback" by its pilots because of the dorsal hump on the fuselage that disturbed the gracious lines of the plane.[7]

---

6   The letters chosen for the patrols had no special meaning, except G for Guards.
7   John Sadler, *Ghost Patrol. A History of the Long Range Desert Group, 1940-1945* (Oxford: Casemate, 2015), p. 41.

The Ghost Patrol was now in the aircraft destruction business. In addition, the patrolmen destroyed one Italian Air Force depot with tons of bombs, and lighted a nice little fire by setting a 32,000 litre petrol tank ablaze. The reactions from the Italians were lame.[8] No counterattack, not even any movements, just some badly aimed rifle fire that caused no bodily harm.

While the explosions were getting all the attention, Bill Kennedy Shaw went up a slope to where the springs supplying 'Ain Zwaya with water were. Some men there who handled the water pumps were captured and brought back for interrogation.[9]

On 25 October, the rest of R Patrol under First Lieutenant Don Steele left Cairo to conduct reconnaissance as far away as Ain Dalla. By 'Uweinat' the patrol mined some roads. Due to mechanical problems, they failed to bring home the hidden Italian trucks. Nevertheless, also LRDG operation No. 2 must be considered a successful one.

Only at the end of November 1940 the Italian Air Force found an opportunity to seek revenge on the LRDG. W Patrol under Captain Teddy Mitford was discovered on November 29 on its way to 'Ain Dua, by an Italian *Sparviero*. The patrol spread out in different directions, according to instructions, when two more aircraft joined in. Their attack lasted for no less than 65 minutes. The Italians started the attack from 300 meters, but as a result of the return fire from the LRDG trucks they rose to 1,500 meters. The Italian crews must have dropped every single bomb they had. However, they caused zero damage. To quote from the action report: "Neither vehicles nor personnel received a single scratch".[10]

How was such bad/good luck possible? Well, it was not only the obvious lack of bombing skills of the *Sparviero* crews that spared W Patrol. The evasion skills of the LRDG drivers probably had more to do with the outcome.[11] Machine gun fire was harder.

How a patrol should act during an air attack depended entirely on the terrain. If it was broken by ravines or consisted of larger blocks of stone, one could instantly take cover and perhaps avoid detection. Or thus still make it difficult for the pilot to hit you. Bombers were, strangely enough, rarely a major danger. Their accuracy at the time was too small. In addition, sand decreased the effect of the explosions. Rocky terrain in some cases was also a bonus for the attacked. Returning fire against attacking aircraft could also stop or disturb pilots.

When the last aircraft had left the area of the attack on W Patrol, the patrolmen emerged, assembled and continued westwards until they found an ideal hideaway in the higher terrain. There W Patrol remained until December 1, when it continued towards the fortress of 'Ain Dua. Once there, with the sun in their backs, the patrol initially found no movement around the fort, but when it fired a Bofors gun from 800 meters, the outpost opened fire with both machine guns and rifles from concealed positions behind walls and rocks.

However, Captain Mitford decided to attack by sending D Troop on foot around the enemy's left flank while the rest of the patrol gave frontal fire support from the cars. The idea was strangely successful, and D Troop forced the enemy's 30 men to abandon their sheltered positions and retreat up a slope.

As Mitford then assumed that Italian combat aircraft were on their way, he broke off the attack and ordered the retreat and to take shelter about two kilometres east of 'Ain Dua. Mitford's hunch had been entirely correct. At 10.15, two *Sparviero* arrived, and half an hour later a *Ghibli*. They disappeared in due time, but the patrol was unsure whether it had been discovered or not, and

---

8   Kennedy Shaw, p. 49.
9   Ibid.
10   CAC: Ralph Bagnold, BGND C 12 (vol I): 'Report On OPERATION NO. 3: 23 November: W Patrol LRDG: Major Mitford' dated 16 December 1940, p. 2.
11   Ibid, p. 4.

continued to hide until about 15.00. Then the patrol attacked the Italian fortress a second time, to demonstrate to the enemy that an LRDG patrol could hide in their neighborhood without being detected from the air and then continue its attack as soon as the air support has disappeared. This demonstration would increase the enemy's insecurity and force him to waste valuable aviation fuel on mostly fruitless aerial reconnaissance.[12]

It may seem as if the patrolmen had a very dramatic existence but an average day in the LRDG, even deep behind enemy lines, actually looked something like this:

Before sunrise, the cook lit the fire while the others could rest a bit more and gaze a few minutes at the eastern horizon brightening and the stars fade. This was the most pleasant time of the day, you were awake but could lie and philosophize, or just enjoy the sky. Then the cook would shout: come and get it! And the porridge was there with one and a half sausage and tea, army biscuits with "margarine with butter contents" (the butter percentage not indicated) and jam.[13]

After breakfast, you cleaned your mug with sand, which in the southern sandstone terrain was easy, but stickier in the north with its limestone terrain.

After cleaning dishes, things could get a bit lazy as there often could be little activity before the sun reached 20 degrees or so across the horizon. A sharp shadow on the solar compass was needed. Without that shadow one would often just stay put and wait.

When the navigators had their information and thus the position, it was time for everyone to move off and the unit would drive in a flight-safe formation, with an aircraft observer on top of the load in each vehicle. It was a bit cold at the start of the day, so you usually wore your greatcoat or even warmer kapok-lined heavy canvas "Tropal coat" (made for operations in places like Norway) and on top a warm cap of some kind.[14] After nine o clock it was time to switch to more sun-protective headgear of some kind, and now it started to quickly get hot. When the sun stood right up in the sky and the shadow was too short for the sun compass, there was an excuse for a rest.

If the enemy was really far away and camouflage was not needed, only a tarpaulin was raised between two cars, which gave a good shadow, and now it was time for a siesta. The patrolmen attempted to avoid sweating, because the sweat dried as soon as it had penetrated, and too much fluid was poured out. You simply rested, talked a little, and the inevitable and never-ending conversation topic was of course water. Swimming in the bathhouse at home, small lakes you had visited, or just a swimming pool. Maybe a bath tub, if you had been lucky enough to grow up with such a thing. Which far from everyone in the LRDG had.

But everyone was not able to rest. The radio operator listened if headquarters had a message and through the smoke-colored lens of his theodolite the navigator checked the sun's journey across the sky towards the meridian.

At one o'clock, the solar compass began to work again and the patrol returned to work, which usually consisted of continuing to move towards some remote destination. However, that did not mean a stop in the search for hostile aircraft.

If the morning minutes were the most beautiful and pleasant in the daytime, the afternoon after three o'clock was the second nicest time of the day. It was noticeably less hot then, and if you then found yourself in the desert of Sirte you could even feel a breeze from the Mediterranean.

In the twilight the patrols preferred to camp in a low-lying place. Low, so as to hide the light from the cooking, and other light sources. It should preferably be a place with soft sand for a comfortable night and good cleaning of the kitchen stuff. Then it was time for the dinner meal

---

12   CAC: Ralph Bagnold, BGND C 12 (vol I): 'Report On OPERATION NO. 3: 23 November: W Patrol LRDG: Major Mitford' dated 16 December 1940, p. 3.
13   Kennedy Shaw, p. 88.
14   Moreman, p. 24.

– hot bully stew, tea and a tot of rum. Then it was time for handing out tomorrow's water ration from the four-gallon containers. You could almost always listen to the eight o'clock news from the BBC, and after settling into a place in the sand, you could fall asleep to the hammer sounds from the mechanics who fixed the day's small and large breakdowns. Small meant that the vehicle could move on its own, major problems meant that the vehicle might be towed during a day or more.

Perhaps, during the night, you might listen to the sound of the radio operator's key going tap-tap-tap, or the navigator's word to the man who would record hour, minute and second in Greenwich time: coming ... coming ... and then the eagerly awaited word *up!* when the desired star entered the hair cross on the theodolite.

In other words, you ought not to be a cook, mechanic, radio operator or navigator if you wanted maximum night sleep. Those specialists would always sleep less than the rest. Still, it was never a problem to find volunteers for any job within the LRDG.

LRDG-meals and cooking

In the LRDG Training Notes one finds instructions for meal routines during operations:

Breakfast: Hot meal, 1 pint [0.57 litres] tea, and 2 pints of water per man to be kept in the water bottle and sipped at any time during the day.

Elevens: Biscuits and dried fruit or chocolate.

Dinner: Soon after midday. Cold meal. 1 pint of water and lime juice or lemon squash.

Supper: Hot meal. 1 pint of tea. Later a further pint of either tea or water.

Firing: Two firing methods are available. When there is no danger of open flames being visible to the enemy, a 4 gallon tin [flimsy] is used as a fire-pot and empty [wooden] petrol cases supply the fuel. Each half-patrol carries two round 2-gallon pots which can be lowered into the fire-pot. This method is simpler and far quicker than the primus [a portable pressurized burner stove from Sweden] method. When open flames might be visible to the enemy, 3-burner primuses are used.

Cooking: Except when camping at a water-hole, no extra water is available for cooking purposes only. Tinned food is heated up by standing the tins (from which the paper wrapping [the labels] has been removed) in the water which is to be used for making tea. The period of actual boiling must be reduced to an absolute minimum in order to save water. Food can also be fried. One frying pan is provided per half-patrol.

Cleaning of utensils etc.: The intense dryness causes food remains (especially syrup from tinned fruit, tea dregs etc.) to solidify so much that it has to be chipped off. All utensils used for food must be cleaned in sand immediately after use, [meaning sand from] drifts of blown sand, not the dried clay of the desert floor.[15]

---

15   CAC: Ralph Bagnold, BGND C 13 (vol II): 'Sheet 8-9: Long Range Desert Group: TRAINING NOTES: RATIONS, MESSING, WATER ETC' undated.

Benito Mussolini's divisions up at Sidi Barrani were near a full-scale disaster in December 1940, and Italy's situation in southern Libya was, mildly put, confused. In the south the culprit was a certain British desert unit based on civilian trucks.

Although Mussolini possessed many desert forts and had many army and air force units in the desert, including "Auto-Saharan" companies – desert specialists of his own (more about them later), things were going badly for him. Apparently, the Italian generals just did not understand what was going on. General Wavell bluffed with his really weak forces, not least by letting the LRDG turn up here and there. Before the Italians had understood the extent of the bluff, the game would be over for them, along with Italy's colonial dreams. Germany's trump card, General Erwin Rommel, however, would considerably prolong the battle for North Africa.

A Chevrolet WB, the first principal LRDG patrol truck, forming part of a desert home for patrolmen. (Estate of Arthur Job via the LRDG Preservation Society)

5

The Murzuk Raid

As a consequence of the fall of France in June 1940, most of the French colonies also ended up on the Axis side of the new world. But already in August 1940, a French territory in Africa, Chad, signaled that it wanted to join the French resistance general, Charles de Gaulle. From England he had raised the banner of opposition to Hitler's occupation of France, and also the French Vichy government, ruling over southern France and the colonies of France.

When General de Gaulle visited Chad in October, the younger officers there showed great enthusiasm for de Gaulle´s cause. When Ralph Bagnold, a month later, met up with Colonel Jean d'Ornano in Fort Lamy, Chad, they immediately understood each other and decided to join forces against the main oasis town in the Libyan province of Fezzan, Murzuk. Previously it had been an important focal point for North African trade. Here the former caravan roads converged.[1]

By themselves, the French forces in Chad and the LRDG did not have the muscles and logistics to cope with an ambitious offensive. Together it was worth a try. At the same time, a raid against Murzuk would also serve as training for an even more important goal, the Kufra Oasis, a perfect starting point for LRDG patrols deeper into Libya's Cyrenaica province.[2]

A successful Murzuk raid would further increase Italian fears for all of southern Libya, and it would most certainly encourage all kinds of French resistance. A British-French success would also counteract the hostile French moods that arose through operation "Catapult", the British attack on the French Navy in Algeria on 3 July, 1940, at its base at Mers-el-Kébir. This was done so that the ships would not fall into Germans hands. But nearly 1,300 French seamen were killed. Due to this the relationship between the French and British reached a new low.

Now the world, especially other French colonies, would hopefully note that the Free French forces (de Gaulle´s forces) in Equatorial Africa did not intend to let the grass grow underneath their feet.

Before Bagnold left Fort Lamy, he and Colonel d'Ornano had of course come up with a bold plan. The Murzuk Oasis was not only some palm trees around a waterhole, but a town with thousands of inhabitants, with a small but modern stone fort, an airfield with some aircraft, and a garrison with about 50 Italian and maybe 150 native soldiers. Previously, there had also been a *Sahariane*-detachment, the Italian equivalent of the LRDG, stationed in Murzuk. Now it was in Cairo, as it had been captured at Sidi Barrani the month before.

The outlook of the LRDG in late 1940 was summarized like this in a report by Bagnold:

By December [1940] the main purpose of the LRDG in Eastern Libya had been achieved. The attention of the enemy had been appreciably distracted from the decisive battle area in the North. It was therefore decided to stir up the sleepy garrisons in the Fezzan, far away in

---

1   *Special Forces in the Desert War 1940-43*, p. 37.
2   Kennedy Shaw, p. 68.

South-Western Libya, where, since the armistice with the French in West Africa, the enemy felt themselves undoubtedly secure.[3]

"One of the strangest journeys ever"

During the Christmas of 1940 the recently established G Patrol under the command of Michael Crichton-Stuart left Cairo along with the more experienced T Patrol under Pat Clayton, who commanded the entire force. Clayton was not just one of the LRDG founders, he looked a lot like Bagnold (born even the same month as him, April 1896) and had the same deep fascination with deserts. To again quote Bagnold:

Clayton […] set out on one of the strangest journeys ever undertaken in war, with no less an object than to cross enemy Libya from end to end and to raid posts 1,200 miles distant from the base. To do this in secret it was necessary to avoid all wells, from which information might leak out, and to navigate a route through unexplored country.[4]

In total, 76 patrolmen set out in 23 vehicles, a remarkable amount for the LRDG, rarely surpassed. In one of them sat the elderly Sheikh 'Abd el Galil Seif en Nasr, scarred after lots of battles against first the Turks, then the Italians. When the Senussi were defeated 10 years earlier, he had fled to Egypt, and his highest wish was to personally kill Italians. His participation in the operation was not a military necessity, but HQ hoped that the Italians would be disturbed by the rumor that the Sheikh was back.

The patrols took the same route across the Great Sand Sea as before. From the depot at Big Cairn they filled petrol and water, and then they continued across the Calanshio Sand Sea to the Kufra trail. They were now far into Libya and still no Italians had observed them, not even from the air. According to the original plan, they would on the way to their main target attack the small Italian outpost at Wau el Kebir. But Pat Clayton then wisely decided to refrain from action, as the large force was still undiscovered and an attack would certainly wake the Italians, perhaps also those at the main destination, Murzuk.

On the tenth day, they were only 160 kilometres from the target. Pat Clayton detached some vehicles from his horde and ordered them to meet the Free French who traveled on petrol-laden camels over the mountains from Bardai.

Waiting for all attack forces to converge, Bill Kennedy Shaw drove around, further mapping the area.

A few days later Clayton arrived with the Free French under the command of Colonel d'Ornano, mounted upon a camel. His turban, flowing robes and monocle against the mysterious backdrop of the region's volcanic peaks made an indelible impression.[5] With him he had only four French officers and five native men, but so many more camels, at first only a few distant dots, but then soundlessly emerging like something from *One Thousand and One Nights*.

On 8 January they rapidly approached Murzuk. The following day, the accompanying sheikh, who had so far been quite loud, was silent and sad. It turned out that they were passing a place

3   CAC: Ralph Bagnold, BGND C 13 (vol II): 'THE WORK OF THE LONG RANGE DESERT GROUP' dated 12 February 1941, p. 4.
4   Ibid.
5   The flowing robes and volcanic peaks made such an impression that they were mentioned in: CAC: Ralph Bagnold, BGND C 13 (vol II): 'THE WORK OF THE LONG RANGE DESERT GROUP' dated 12 February 1941, p. 5.

where the Italians had shot 11 of his clan members. For Bedouins, every place, even the seemingly empty, has a story to tell.

Without drama, the Allied raiding force reached the outskirts of Murzuk early in the morning of 11 January 1941.[6] Behind a mighty curtain of palms, the white dome of the Murzuk mosque was sighted. On one side was the fort with its high radio mast. On the other side, a bit further away, were the contours of the aircraft hangar and behind it a vast sand sea. As no enemy forces had yet emerged the raiders decided to mine the road and then eat a solid lunch.

While this was going on the sentry reported aircraft. There was a moment of despair that the force should be discovered at the last minute of the eleventh hour, but, it was only a bomber returning from a flight.

When everyone had eaten, they drove the final three kilometres of the 2,400 kilometre journey from Cairo. Pat Clayton led the force from his 15-cwt, then came Sergeant Cyril Hewson in a 30-cwt from T Patrol, and lastly the line of G Patrol cars. This procession was so impressive that it actually rendered Fascist greetings from a group of soldiers standing by the roadside. They obviously assumed that the force was Italian.[7]

An Italian postmaster, Signor Coliccia, was cycling towards the Murzuk fort when Pat Clayton just grabbed him from his bike, and placed him in his car. Signor Coliccia was promptly made to act as a guide of the attacking force. His bike was also sucked into the car, for later use in Cairo.

At the front of the fort, several men were observed, acting as if nothing in the world could disturb them. But this was just what the force did. Sergeant Hewson turned left with a few T Patrol trucks and opened fire against the fort soldiers, while G Patrol drove to the right and began to fire at the fort itself.

The main part of T Patrol headed for the airfield and the hangar. There they were met by machine gun fire from one of the few Italians who reacted and showed some initiative. This immediately caused a tragic outcome. Colonel d'Ornano, rifle in hand, was struck by a bullet in his throat and died practically immediately, along with an Italian sergeant who also had been forcibly recruited to act as a guide. T Patrol then silenced the machine gun with its Bofors gun.[8]

A group of Italian soldiers fired a few shots from the hangar, until one of them attached a white handkerchief to a pole and waved it. With him about twenty Italians surrendered.

Meanwhile at the fort, Sergeant Hewson was mortally hit, and another three patrolmen were wounded. One of the Bofors rounds against the fort had set a building on fire including its flagstaff with raised flag, a most symbolic sight.

In the midst of fire from both sides, a touring car drove up to the fort gate. An LRDG Bofors shell blew it to pieces. Sadly, the car was found to contain not only the Italian fort commander but also his wife and child.[9] The town was no desert battlefield without civilians.

In the hangar the patrolmen found a welcome prize, three *Ghibli* bombers. These Caproni aircraft were the most common type for bombing and aerial reconnaissance in Italy's African colonies, and an export version of it could be found even in such remote countries as Peru, Norway and Sweden. Strangely enough the just captured aircraft had British Lewis machine guns. Bill Kennedy Shaw remarked about this in his memoirs: "Such are the mysteries of the international armaments business."[10] But the explanation was that Italy had previously been a British ally. Britain

6   *Special Forces in the Desert War 1940-43*, p. 38.
7   One might surmise that these troops were indigenous, but Bagnold's 1941 report states: "The few Italian soldiers passed on the outskirts raised their hands in the Fascist salute." Source: CAC: Ralph Bagnold, BGND C 13 (vol II): 'THE WORK OF THE LONG RANGE DESERT GROUP' dated 12 February 1941, p. 5.
8   Kennedy Shaw, p. 61.
9   Kennedy Shaw, p. 61.
10   Ibid.

had even ordered fighter aircraft from Italy shortly before the outbreak of the Second World War. They were never delivered.

From the twenty or so sullen Italian prisoners Pat Clayton picked out the four who seemed the brightest. The rest were let free, to the French participants' big disappointment. They'd rather have cut their throats.

The Libyan prisoners were ordered to pump petrol over the aircraft. As a fuse, a string of fuel was poured into the hangar gate. A match was lighted. The Allied force barely had left the airfield when the explosions shook the hangar, the flames licked the walls and the roof fell over the three airplanes. In 1968, LRDG veteran David Lloyd Owen was again in Murzuk and found that the remains of the Italian Second World War aircraft were still where they were once destroyed by the LRDG. Bits and pieces of the aircraft were still around the airfield forty years after Lloyd Owen's visit, as can be seen in the 2009 New Zealand TV documentary "Lost in Libya".

The raiders left Murzuk the same way as they had arrived, and in the chilly wind that blew outside the city, they buried Hewson and d'Ornano.

The countrymen of the Italian prisoners did not make any effort to pursue the force, despite the fact that they by now ought to be aware of both the limited number of Allied troops and that they mostly had just light weapons.

Speaking of the prisoners, one of them, in the twilight, fell off the vehicle he was sitting in, without anyone noticing. But the man ran and caught up with his British hosts. This must have amused Bagnold, who wrote about it in his report, thus: "one fell off the back of a truck at the moment of departure and dutifully started running after it to avoid being left behind."[11]

Towards Chad

Having reached Murzuk and accomplished their tasks there, T and G Patrols now steered from southwest Libya to Chad, the first French colony to rejoin the Allies (on August 26 1940) after the military defeat of France. On the way there the basic idea was that the LRDG should be as much of a nuisance as possible. For success, a lot depended on if the Italian outposts along the route had been in touch with Murzuk via radio. Some might still be unaware of the existence of the raiding force in their area.

First the patrols came to the small town of Traghen. There the group of prisoners of war was expanded with two camel-riding policemen. Pat Clayton ordered one of them to enter the local fort with the task of inviting the garrison to surrender within twenty minutes. If not, it would be very sad for them, when the Bofors canons would take over the negotiating. Twenty minutes had not yet passed when a lot of noise was heard from within the fort, shooting and drumming.

Prepared for an attack from the fort, the patrols readied themselves. But instead, the gate was opened in an open and peaceful manner, and out wandered a procession of flying flags, drums and the local boss. Behind it followed two dispirited *carabinieri*, Italian paramilitary police, and the rest of the garrison. But, Traghen surrendered in style. Women and children joined in and strengthened the noise when the procession came out on the main street.[12]

Pat Clayton, Bill Kennedy Shaw and Michael Crichton-Stuart entered the big gate into the fort, where the surrender procedure continued with the Italians handing over two machine guns, a number of rifles, an Italian flag and a typewriter along with a huge amount of documents. When the stacks were studied in the evening, the patrolmen realized that the Italian Army was even more

11   CAC: Ralph Bagnold, BGND C 13 (vol II): 'THE WORK OF THE LONG RANGE DESERT GROUP' dated 12 February 1941, p. 5.
12   *Special Forces in the Desert War 1940-43*, p. 38; Kennedy Shaw, p. 64.

fond of paperwork than the War Office. Kennedy Shaw knew Italian and sat up half the night studying forms, manuals to fill out the forms and manuals to understand the manuals. The best one was a tutorial on how to use a bicycle, with wonderfully serious instructions. More useful information was obtained from the prisoners already taken in Murzuk, and the force left Traghen without adding more prisoners. Space in the vehicles was now very limited, as was the food, petrol and water.

Traghen had been an easy job, but harder tasks lay ahead. First, on to Umm el Araneb. Even from far away the patrolmen could see that this outpost had a large radio antenna, so the men inside were probably forewarned. There remained no doubt after Pat Clayton sent off his prisoner-postmaster to communicate demands, the poor man quickly returned with machine gun bullets whistling about his ears. With no armoured vehicles and no gun with a calibre more than 37mm, it would be a bloody affair to storm this well-designed fort surrounded by sloping sides consisting of soft sand. No point in trying, instead the force continued towards Gatrun and Tejerri.

Clayton had previously made an arrangement with a company of *Méhariste*, French camel riders from the *Groupe Nomade de Tibesti*, that they, from Tummo, on the Chad-Libya border, would attack Tejerri on 14 January together with the LRDG. But there, too, the local garrison was on its guard and willing to fight. The LRDG's attempt to co-operate with the camel company had also failed. Without a radio connection between them, they simply did not find each other in the desert. Much later it became known that *Méhariste's* solo attack against Tejerri also came to nothing. Their guides were from the Tibbu tribe, which was moderately interested in getting new Europeans at their doorstep. The tribe preferred the status quo and simply led the company of *Méhariste* in the wrong direction.

The men in the LRDG considered themselves tough and hardy, and they certainly were. But those who had the opportunity to compare their life with that of the *Méhariste* in Chad must have been humbled. Without anything but a blanket to lay on the ground, these Frenchmen could be on assignment for months in a row from the already primitive life of a desert posting. In comparison, LRDG patrolmen would after some tough weeks mostly go back to Cairo's delightful civilization. *Méharistes* must always follow their camels that needed the changing and lean feed of the wilderness. After the attempted joint operation with the British, they could not get back straight home, but had to first search for a place where they knew there might be camel feed, so that they could move on later. In addition, they had been expelled from their own country by the collaborating French Vichy government. After many years of rough living in remote colonies, they were considered lawless.[13]

The only thing *Méhariste* had left was the pride of refusing to cooperate with those who had taken their country.

For the patrol members, the mail was the highlight of the return to Cairo, when the letters from home were distributed. For the Free French officers there was virtually no mail to look forward to, as there was no official postal connection to Chad from German-occupied France, nor from Vichy France. Without the opportunity of contact with their families, they could only hope that France one day would be liberated.

Suddenly, above Clayton's raiders, aircraft from the Italian Air Force, the *Regia Aeronautica*, actually did appear. But their effort was a waste of time. The planes did manage to drop some bombs, but none of them fell even close.

The reunited patrols continued against Zouar in Chad. To save fuel, a shortcut was taken over a corner of Niger. That colony had remained under Vichy when Chad had settled on General de Gaulle. But the border violation went just fine and payed off.

13   Kennedy Shaw, p. 65.

In Zouar, the Free French Captain Massu was a generous host. He had been wounded in the leg by a bullet during the battle of Murzuk, but had himself stopped the bleeding with a glowing cigarette, and then never talked about that matter. He was that kind of man.

The clash at Jebel Sherif

In the morning of 19 January 1941, Ralph Bagnold arrived in Chad in a very outdated French Bloch bomber. As soon as he met a French officer, he asked: "How many vehicles are ready for an attack on Kufra in cooperation with the Free French?" Kufra was truly a key oasis, with caravan roads going in all directions and it could serve as an ideal starting point for future LRDG missions.

After d'Ornano's death, Colonel Philippe Leclerc took charge in Chad. He was actually a member of the noble family de Hautecloque, but had adopted a *nom de guerre* so that his relatives might not have to pay for his success in fighting the Germans. Leclerc had searched the entire province for vehicles in order to equip a force that could conquer Kufra. Now it was decided that Clayton's two patrols would be placed under him before the operation. They were to start from Faya and on the way north also spy on 'Uweinat and the Italian bases there. If the Italians were to place a more mobile force there, it would pose a serious threat to Leclerc's communications.

The Italians must pretty soon have grasped that an attack on Kufra was being planned, because "To Kufra!" had become a sort of local greeting on the streets of Tibesti.

Both patrols left Faya in Chad on 26 January, and five days later Clayton and his T Patrol reached the Jebel Sherif area, a group of hills on a firm and very flat plain, about 130 kilometres southwest of Kufra. G Patrol stayed in reserve by Sarra.

Close to Jebel Sherif, T Patrol was spotted by a *Ghibli* airplane attached to an Italian motorized desert unit. If the LRDG had a counterpart on the Italian side it was the *Autosahariana*-companies (also just *Sahariana*) created by Marshal Graziani a few years before the war.[14] As evident from the formal name of the units, *Auto-Avio-Sahariane*, these companies were intended to have constant air support. It was for this particular cooperation that Caproni designed the *Ghibli* plane.

Now, *Sahariana* tactics and training would be tested against the Brits, seeking protection by hiding in the hills of the Jebel Sherif.

Clayton's patrol consisted of eleven 30-cwt Chevrolets and they clashed with five desert cars belonging to the *Sahariana*-company "Cufra".[15] A crucial difference between the two sides was that the Italians had 20mm Breda anti-aircraft guns, also very effective against ground targets and one of the best weapons Italy has ever made.[16] The Italians also had eyes in the sky, three Italian aircraft were supporting the hunt from above. The Italian fire quickly destroyed three of the LRDG trucks in a valley, and three men were killed: Corporal Beech and two Italians including the postmaster of Murzuk. The British were later accused in Italian newspapers for shooting the prisoners, but they died from Italian guns firing on the LRDG vehicles.

Two other Italians escaped and were later taken care of by their countrymen. Four wounded patrolmen succeeded in finding a shelter in a hillside. Three Italians were killed and several injured from Corporal Beech's machine gun fire. Beech was then himself killed. The rest of Clayton's patrol had escaped the fire and made a turn and were keen to counterattack. However, they were again attacked, by three bomber aircraft. The cars dispersed just as they were supposed to during an air attack, but Clayton's car was damaged, and with two other patrolmen he was taken prisoner.

---

14   Kuno Gross with Roberto Chiarvetto and Brendan O'Carroll, *Incident at Jebel Sherif* (Singapore: Star Standard Industries Ltd, 2009).
15   Gross, p. 97.
16   Moreman, 54.

A Chevrolet WB at a fort, probably during the Murzuk raid. Note the sand mat. (Churchill Archives Centre, Ralph Bagnold, BGND, C12, Vol I, ID: DL 25-206)

LRDG patrolmen discussing or planning with Frenchmen. (Churchill Archives Centre, Ralph Bagnold, BGND, C12, Vol I, ID: E.52)

By visiting the area and years of research by various other means, three LRDG enthusiasts, Kuno Gross, Roberto Chiarvetto and Brendan O'Carroll, came to some interesting conclusions about the clash at Jebel Sherif. For example that the LRDG could have suffered a much heavier blow, had the Italians left just one of their armed trucks at the northern exit of the channel in the hills where the patrolmen were hiding. This mistake allowed the majority of T patrol to escape into the open desert, where they could disperse and make use of the speed advantage they had against the available Italian vehicles.[17]

The seven remaining cars of T Patrol drove southwards, and it was assumed that the rest of the patrol members were either dead or captured. The patrol reached the planned rendezvous at Tecro and there joined up with G Patrol and Colonel Leclerc.

But there remained some patrolmen who had survived the attack and found a good hiding place: Trooper Ronald Moore, Private Alfred Tighe and two Scots Guardsmen, Alexander Winchester and John Easton.[18] They only had the clothes they were wearing, a tin of jam and two gallons of water in a tin with a bullet hole through it.[19] Additionally, they still had responsibility for one of the Italian prisoners of war. Moore had a bad injury in a foot, Easton suffered from a bullet wound in his mouth. They now had two choices: either walk to Kufra and let themselves be captured, or follow the patrol's tracks and hope to be picked up before they died. They chose the latter option.

They covered some sixty kilometres in the first twenty-four hours of their ordeal. Day after day they continued, nearly mad with thirst. During the night they would dig a hole in the sand and lay with their arms around each other. Their Italian prisoner wandered off and was fortunate enough to be picked up, and by his own army too.

On the seventh day of desert walking, Tighe's powers had ended, and he stopped at an old hut. Finding one match in the sand, together with some oil, he was able to light a fire.[20] He was probably right in later assuming that he had been saved by that fire.

Easton pressed on for another day. Then he fell and was unable to get up. Winchester and Moore rubbed his legs to start his circulation, got him to his feet, but he could just stumble and again dropped. Moore gave Easton half of the remaining drops and then continued with Winchester. By now their boots were worn through, so they tramped barefoot over the hot sand. Their spirits were raised when they were discovered by a French airplane. It dropped a bottle for them, which unfortunately had leaked as the cork fell out upon landing. Well, they each got a mouthful.[21]

The Free French patrol that found Tighe could almost read in his face that he had not had any water for four days. Still, Tighe was able to report the plight of his lost comrades to the French, who followed his tracks backwards, and thus found Easton.

Meanwhile, another rescue patrol found Winchester, who also had fallen over, unable to get up again. Moore was somehow able to walk another 16 kilometres before the French patrol caught up with him. When they did, he was still determined to reach the well at Tekro, 130 kilometres further on. After having walked 334 kilometres through the desert with his injured foot, Moore was almost offended by being picked up. His feat is remembered as "Moore's March".[22]

John Easton was the first Scots Guardsman to die in North Africa. But his three evading comrades survived and recovered. Ronald Moore was awarded the Distinguished Conduct Medal

---

17   Gross, p. 110; Mortimer (2015:1), p. 51.
18   Kennedy Shaw, p. 72; Lloyd Owen, p. 35.
19   Kennedy Shaw, p. 72; Morgan, p. 45; Thompson, p. 32.
20   Kennedy Shaw, p. 73; Lloyd Owen, p. 36.
21   Ibid; Ibid; *Special Forces in the Desert War 1940-43*, p. 42; Thompson, p. 32.
22   Gross, p. 112.

for his actions, the first member of the New Zealand Division to receive the award in the Second World War.[23]

The remainder of T Patrol and G Patrol minus one vehicle began the homeward journey on 4 February. One 30-cwt with a navigator and two regular patrolmen was detached to the Free French for reconnaissance in the Kufra area.

Via Kharga the patrols reached Cairo on 9 February. Since leaving Cairo on 26 December, they had traveled about 7,200 kilometres. Their total losses amounted to two killed in action and four missing, of which three later returned, and they brought three prisoners back with them. Four 30-cwt had been destroyed by the Italians and two had been lost due to mechanical problems. The Italians were so delighted, that the newspaper founded by Mussolini, *Il Popolo d´Italia* (The People of Italy), exclaimed: "The capture of Klayton [sic] was a master-stroke".[24]

Losing Clayton was indeed serious for the LRDG, for not only was he an LRDG founder very much at ease in the desert environment, he also had on him the plans for the next Allied moves in the area.[25] But capturing these documents did not change the Italian luck.

What about Moore´s and his comrades´ incredible marching feat? Was the decision to not surrender to the Italians not quite mad, considering the tiny amount of water they had? Well, going back would bring them to their pre-arranged rendezvous, where at least one T patrol vehicle was thought to be waiting for them, or at least some water. Also, G patrol was supposed to be moving in their direction, along the route they followed back. So, of course the march was a major feat, but the participants had not imagined they would have to do so much walking.[26]

Patrolmen and Frenchmen after Murzuk, second from the right could be Pat Clayton. A captured bicycle from the Murzuk raid and just below the bike a sand mat on the closest truck. (Estate of Arthur Job via LRDG Preservation Society)

23   Lloyd Owen, p 37.
24   Gavin Mortimer, *The Long Range Desert Group in World War II* (Oxford: Osprey, 2017), p. 69; Sadler, p. 47.
25   Mortimer (2017), p. 41.
26   Gross, p. 112.

Part of T patrol waiting for the fort of Traghen to capitulate, on 12 January 1941. In the background Chevrolets and just in front of the camera a Ford 01 V8 15-cwt called "TE RANGI", maori for chief (also on p.28 & 44). Behind the Vickers machine gun is Vice Corporal Lawrence "Clarrie" Roderick, a pro boxer. Shortly after the photo was taken he was in combat and was captured and sent to a POW camp in Italy. He escaped and joined the partisans, fighting with them to his death in 1944. The photographer was F. Jopling. (Alexander Turnbull Library, Wellington, N.Z. bildnr DA-00872)

This wartime painting shows LRDG patrolmen in Arab headdress and sandals with three Chevrolets in the background. The artist, Captain Peter McIntyre, was an official New Zealand war painter in Africa and later in Europe. He called this painting "Beyond the Great Sand Sea". (Archives New Zealand War Art collection, ref. AAAC 898 NCWA 3)

Beards were a common sight in the Ghost Patrol. Note the sand mat just below the driver's head. The inside of the mats were painted in the British colours and thus the mats had a dual purpose – to get unstuck and to let friendly aircraft understand that the truck was friendly. NZ war artist Peter McIntyre called this painting "LRDG Kiwis". (Archives New Zealand War Art collection, ref. AAAC 898 NCWA 18)

A Chevrolet 1533X2 30 cwt, classic workhorse of the LRDG. Note the Nya Zeland national symbol on the hood and name "TIRAU II", Maori for a NZ tree. "TIRAU II" belonged to T1 patrol and took part in the Barce raid, when it was destroyed. This replica sports a capured German MG 34 in the rear. The LRDG used various captured weapons. (LRDG Preservation Society)

The same Chevrolet 1533X2 30 cwt up front.
(LRDG Preservation Society)

The SAS in early 1942 started using the classic American Jeep but were forced to abandon some. These were then picked up by the LRDG and became the first jeeps of the unit. This replica shows an LRDG jeep, the difference being very slight. Usually SAS vehicles had one or two more machine guns. (LRDG Preservation Society)

The LRDG Chevrolet WB that was recovered from the desert in 1983. Its markings identify it as truck No. 8 of W Patrol, disbanded in December 1940. The patrol's vehicles were redistributed to the newly created G (Guards) Patrol. The vehicle was lost either in late 1940 by W Patrol or early/mid 1941 when operated by G Patrol before they had chance to update the markings. The trucks had Maori nicknames. This one was named by Trooper Clarkie Waetford as "WAIKAHA", where his family came from. This photo was taken while it was preserved in Wales, displayed in a desert scenery complete with flimsies in the sand. Since many years it is in the Imperial War Museum in London. (Lars Gyllenhaal)

Up close the Maori name "WAIKAHA" is still visible on the side of the Chevrolet´s bonnet. (Graham Bould)

The truck's patrol designation (W) is a bit more visible on the side of body, in front of the driver's seat. All trucks in W Patrol were given Maori names starting with a W. (Graham Bould)

Close-up of the British flag insignia on the tailgate of "WAIKAHA" on permanent display at the Imperial War Museum. (Graham Bould)

The team in the Egyptian desert, from the left: Mahmud, Jason, Karl-Gunnar, Rick, Sam, Bob and John. (Karl-Gunnar Norén)

Many desert expeditions were planned in this house in Cairo, where Pat Clayton lived. (Karl-Gunnar Norén)

Karl-Gunnar Norén in the Jeep, wearing original British Second World War (desert) windproof trousers. (Toby Savage)

Flimsies, flimsies! Yes, from the war and still there. (Karl-Gunnar Norén)

Just like that, in the middle of nowhere, we found this Second World War spade made in Australia. (Karl-Gunnar Norén)

The parts of the cans that have not been exposed are in remarkably good condition. We found a milk (evaporated type) can labeled: "Nestle 1942" and a tin of British Army corned beef from Argentina. (Karl-Gunnar Norén)

Documenting the remains of a Chevrolet engine, probably from a 1939 Egyptian or 1942 Canadian built one. (Karl-Gunnar Norén)

Sergeant Sam Watson at the "WAIKAHA" discovery site. (Karl-Gunnar Norén)

One of our desert camps. Soon after this time the stars appear. We are so far away from all human light sources.
(Karl-Gunnar Norén)

The overturned Ford from 1942 that we found, by chance. (Karl-Gunnar Norén)

Inspecting the Ford and the air is filled with technical and historical comments. Exciting! (Karl-Gunnar Norén)

At the LRDG airfield at Gilf Kebir. Air petrol flimsies that have surely been used to fill up WACO aircraft. (Karl-Gunnar Norén)

Toby and Rick with the third truck that week we found, a CMP Ford. (Karl-Gunnar Norén)

Our expedition crosses tracks from the Sudan trade route. (Karl-Gunnar Norén)

This CMP 4x4 Ford from the LRDG Rhodesian S Patrol was left here in April 1941 due to a broken steering column. (Karl-Gunnar Norén)

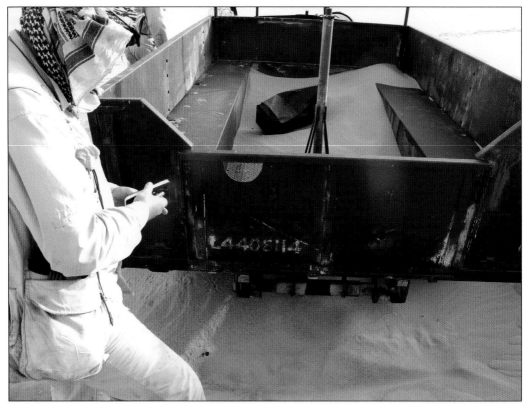

It was great to find not only paint on an LRDG Ford, but also a painted number – not far from the number of the Bofors truck that was inspected by General Auchinleck (in the previous book section). (Karl-Gunnar Norén)

Karl-Gunnar behind the wheel. (John Carroll)

We have travelled through the Great Sand Sea and reached Siwa! (Karl-Gunnar Norén)

The very last photograph of Bill "Swede" Anderson was this one, taken in October 1999 in the SAS barracks with a LRDG Jeep reminding him of his desert days. (Peter Anderson and David Hall)

The LRDG has fans all over the world and is commemorated in various ways, not least by scale modellers. Here a radio version of a LRDG Chevrolet 1533X2 30-cwt truck in a 1/35 scale desert diorama by Erik Ahlström. The kit is from Tamiya but has many additional details. (Erik Ahlström)

A Ford/Marmon-Herrington truck from the LRDG Heavy Section. These trucks sported British standard camouflage while the other LRDG vehicles at first had a camouflage pattern of light stone and purple brown. It was more or less scratch built in 1/35 scale by using various bits and pieces from several kits and plastic card. The project started with a photograph. (Erik Ahlström)

LRDG Jeep with sun compass and Browning .303 machine gun from the RAF and carrying an air recognition roundel on the bonnet. This 1/35 scale model started with a Tamiya kit. Again, the project was based on a wartime photo. (Erik Ahlström)

Lars Gyllenhaal in Cairo in what was once General Headquarters, Middle East, in the Cairo Citadel. Now it is i.a. the Egyptian National Military Museum. The tank closest to the author, a former tank commander, is a Soviet Josef Stalin tank. (Ann-Sofie Gyllenhaal)

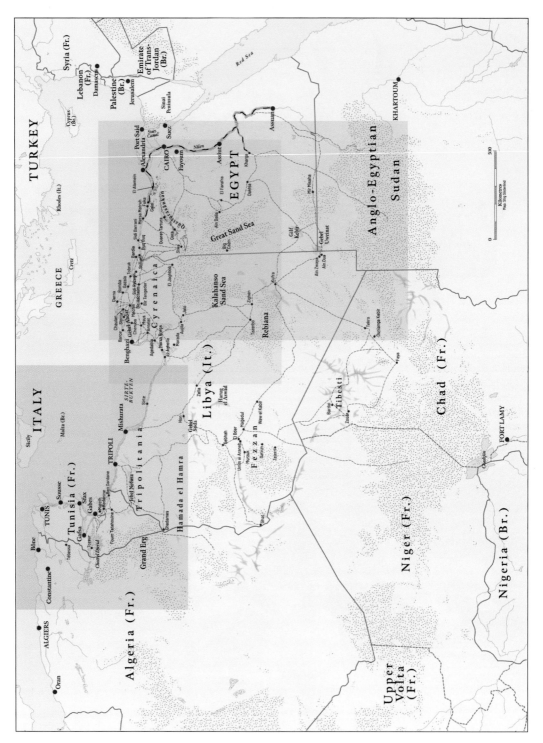

Map 1: Overview, LRDG area of operations 1940-43

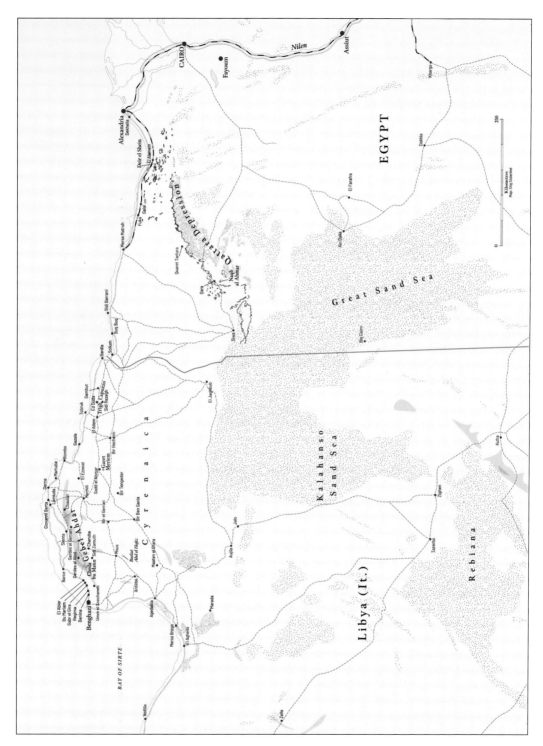

Map 2: Libya and Egypt

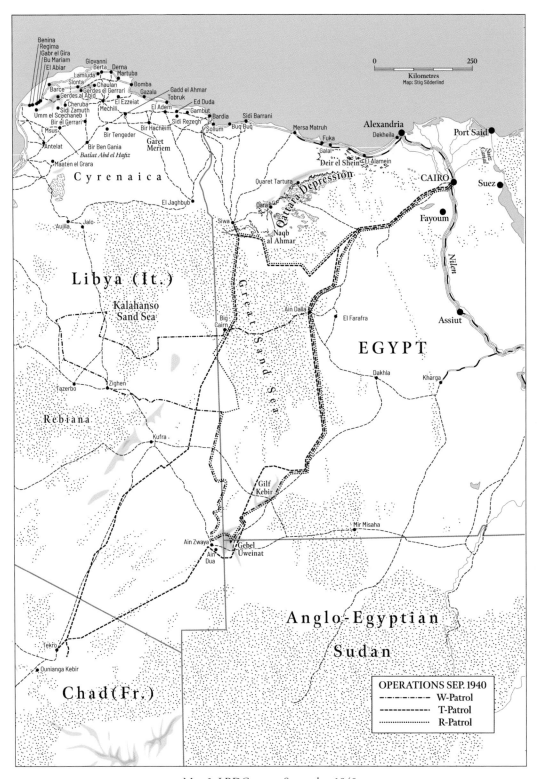

Map 3: LRDG routes September 1940

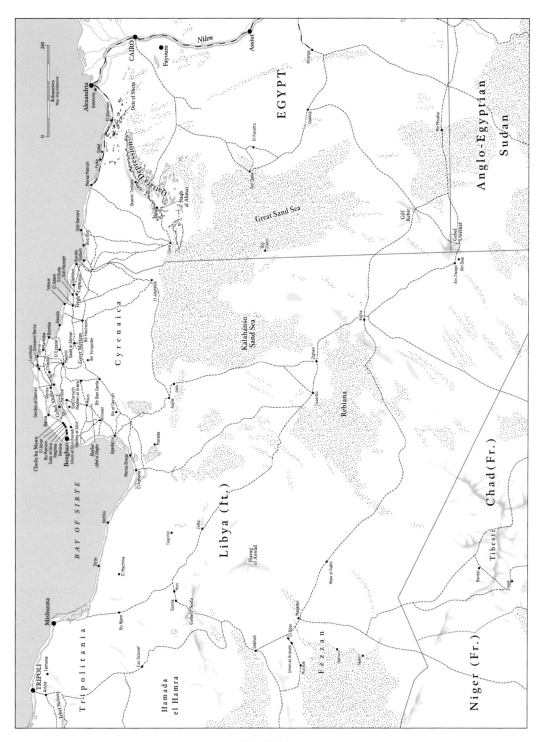

Map 4: Libya

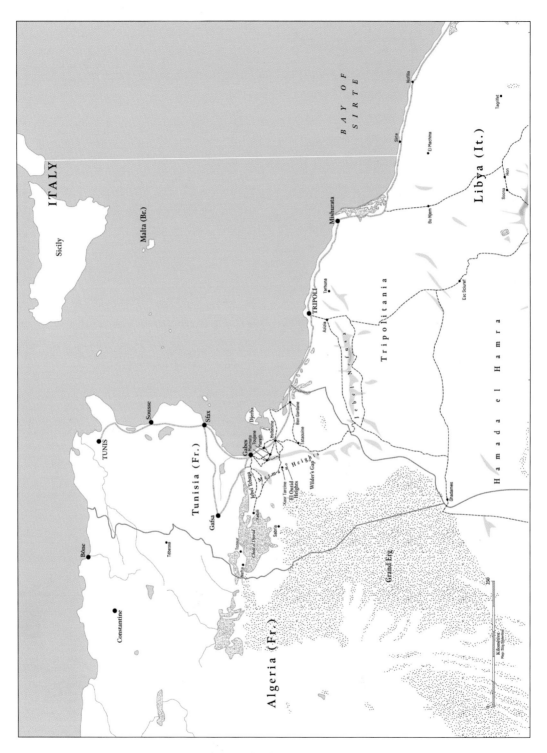

Map 5: Wilder's Gap in Tunisia

6

Kufra and the "LRDG Air Force"

With the fall of Benghazi on 6 February 1941, Libyan Cyrenaica was fully in Allied hands. Wavell's offensive, which started as a reconnaissance in force, had evolved into an unprecedented destruction of Italian war machinery. On paper, Italy had impressive fighting forces in North Africa. But Marshal Rodolfo Graziani had completely misunderstood the development of desert tactics that had taken place. The main goal was now *not* to conquer a position or a piece of land, but to hit as many enemy vehicles and fuel dumps as possible.[1] Even the most modern and brilliant army will come to a standstill without fuel.

Here Bagnold's thinking fitted the situation like hand in glove. The piracy he had offered General Wavell in 1940 was basically about preventing enemy troops from moving by stopping their engines, and also forcing the enemy to divert resources like troops, aircraft and trucks to defend roads and positions far from the frontline. So, the LRDG was in demand more than ever. In early 1941 Bagnold wrote a report, probably with some pride, that summed up the effect his unit had so far had:

> Throughout the whole length and breadth of Libya the Italians have for months past been kept on the alert; of how they have been made to expend petrol, aircraft and transport in protecting their desert garrisons; of how phantom British motor columns have appeared like the Will 'o the Wisp now here, now there, now at several places at once, sometimes close to the Egyptian frontier, sometimes a thousand miles away in the West; pirating transport on the roads, shelling and capturing isolated forts, blowing up dumps and burning aircraft on the ground. [...] That well-armed parties of troops have made journeys of several thousand miles through enemy territory carrying with them their own supplies of petrol, food and even of water to last them for many weeks at a time; constitutes something quite new in military history.[2]

However, by the end of January, 1941 it was clear that the fleet of 30-cwt Chevrolet trucks were pretty worn and could not handle much more because of the extra friction that desert use entails. Sadly, there were no equivalent vehicles available throughout the Middle East, and the War Office's position was to drop all 30-cwt. A small but insufficient boost in anticipation of new vehicles was a dozen Fiat SPA AS.37 *Sahariano*. They were part of the spoils from the Battle of Bardia. When they worked, they were excellent, but they were just not trustworthy, they broke down time after time. Raiding with such problematic vehicles against remote targets was not a good idea.

---

1   CAC: Ralph Bagnold, BGND C 13 (vol II): 'THE WORK OF THE LONG RANGE DESERT GROUP' dated 12 February 1941, p. 1.
2   CAC: Ralph Bagnold, BGND C 13 (vol II): 'THE WORK OF THE LONG RANGE DESERT GROUP' dated 12 February 1941, p. 1.

LRDG emblem and clothing

According to the legend, the LRDG beret badge, a scorpion inside a wheel, came about when the New Zealand navigator of R2 Patrol. Gunner "Bluey" Grimsey, was stung by a scorpion, and not just once but thrice.[3] After such an attack one might think that there were some bad consequences for Grimsey, but instead it was the scorpion that died.[4] Accordingly, the dead scorpion became Grimsey's personal symbol of luck. He then got the idea of making a brooch with the symbol for his girlfriend spread, and that idea spread within the unit. The emblem was thus first made on private initiative by some of Cairo's jewelry stores.[5]

However, there exists another, and perhaps more true, story to explain what became the main symbol of the LRDG. According to Teddy Mitford, he had himself before the war observed some Italian biplanes with a scorpion inside a wheel on their fuselage.[6] Upon joining the LRDG Mitford then suggested to Bagnold that a scorpion should be the badge of the unit. After an OK Mitford then had "Bluey" Grimsey, who was one of his soldiers, properly design it.[7]

The scorpion badge was combined with a black tanker beret from the Royal Armoured Corps, and thus the semi-official headdress of the LRDG was created. The badge was made in a number of varieties and qualities. The color can be silver, brass or bronze and separating originals from replicas is an art in itself.

After the assignment in Africa, the LRDG got the same berets as the SAS, then sand colored. But this did not mean that the black beret immediately disappeared, and berets were far from the only headdress within the unit. In addition to the fact that some insisted on wearing the hats of their old units, at least sometimes, patrolmen often wore wool caps or traditional Arab headgear, *keffiyeh*, which were ideal for protection from sand and sun.

Of course, the strong sun and the desert dust made it necessary to often wear goggles of some sort.

The uniforms showed that patrolmen came from various units. During assignment wide and airy desert shorts was standard, but the patrolman was free to compose his clothing according to season, weather and personal taste.[8] On the feet, you had either regular British army boots or sandals. In total, the LRDG look was highly personal, and thus it was sometimes hard to believe that a patrol was actually not a group of archaeologists or explorers. Which in some cases also happened to be true.

One piece of LRDG insignia was added, black slip-on shoulder titles with "LRDG" in red letters. Far from all patrolmen wore them, though. Those who did discovered that the sun transformed the red letters to pink. Standard khaki drill epaulettes could also be modified by adding "LRDG" stenciled in black letters.[9] Some LRDG men were trained in parachute jumping by the SAS and after having qualified wore SAS jump wings above the left chest pocket.

3   Len Whittaker, *Some Talk of Private Armies* (Harpenden: Albanium Publishing, 1984), p. 19.
4   Jenner & List, p. 39; Mortimer (2015:1), p. 85.
5   For one of the earliest examples (perhaps the very first type), with both "LRP" and "LRDG" below the scorpion, see Gross, p. 19.
6   Mortimer (2015:1), p. 85.
7   Ibid, p. 86.
8   Moreman, p. 23.
9   Whittaker, p. 19.

Black LRDG (tanker) beret with LRDG scorpion insignia and slip-on shoulder titles. As the LRDG was a small unit, original LRDG insignia is rare – but there are replicas, such as these. (Lars Gyllenhaal)

But there was a small opening: the Canadian Army had ordered a number of four-wheel drive 30-cwt Ford trucks with V8 engines, that were already in Egypt. However, they could not be used because they all suffered from a mechanical problem. They were pretty ordinary army trucks, called CMP, for Canadian Military Pattern. But without their roofs and doors, they might not differ significantly from the 30-cwt Chevrolets?

Bagnold understood that there would be problems with the Ford CMPs. He also knew that the patrols' action radius would now drastically decrease. But he had no other choice than to accept 70 of the new vehicles. By 20 March the known faults had been remedied and modifications had also been made to his specifications. Ceilings, windows and doors had been cut and special weapon mounts added. Now the LRDG vehicle fleet was at full strength again.

LRDG based in Kufra

The Free French under Colonel Leclerc took Kufra from Mussolini on 1 March 1941. This was excellent news for not only French resistance everywhere but especially for the LRDG. When the British completed the conquest of Libyan Cyrenaica at the end of February 1941, and took aim at northwestern Libya, Tripolitania, it was not very convenient for the LRDG to be based in Cairo. It was natural to continue the cooperation with the Free French forces and to firmly establish the LRDG in Kufra. This would also strengthen the French ability to repel Italian attempts at recapturing the place. Kufra was Cyrenaica's central oasis where many caravan routes met.

Bagnold decided to quickly get to Kufra with the new S Patrol, which consisted of recruits from South Rhodesia. On 9 March the patrol was ready for departure from Cairo. The operation had several purposes. Before the British based troops in a new location, it was important for them to take a doctor to the place, to assess the disease state, especially the malaria status. That's why "Doc" Lawson, LRDG's own doctor, also came along, in his own car.[10] It was a 15-cwt Ford, then still fully open and thus offering wounded no protection from the wind and sand. Lawson was definitely brave. He would receive an MC, Military Cross, for protecting wounded with his own body when they were being shot at from an attacking aircraft.[11]

The British Army also needed to establish a reliable radio station to create a stable and secure connection with Cairo. The patrol thus brought with them equipment that could be connected to the excellent masts the Italians had left behind.[12]

This mission also offered ultimate training for both newly arrived replacements, and for the unexperienced S Patrol. General Freyberg had denied the continued use of New Zealand volunteers, but it turned out that South Rhodesia could offer men who had roughly the same background as the New Zealanders.

The force took the old route to Kufra Oasis, from Cairo to 'Ain Dalla, across the Great Sand Sea to Big Cairn and then southwestwards. After 10 days of travel, they sighted the first palm grove belonging to Kufra.

The first impression of Kufra was unforgettable. Before Fascist Italy conquered the oasis, it was a distant, mysterious place with no regular connections. A real must for every desert enthusiast. Like many oases in the Libyan desert, it is at the foot of an east-west steep incline, hollowed by the wind during thousands of years. The terrain slopes down to the water magically pouring from the underworld. Now, in principle, there is no rainfall in the interior of Libya's deserts. The theory that seems to be most supported among scientists is that rain falling over the Tibesti Mountains/

10   Lloyd Owen, p. 128.
11   Ibid, p. 113.
12   *Special Forces in the Desert War 1940-43*, pp. 48-49.

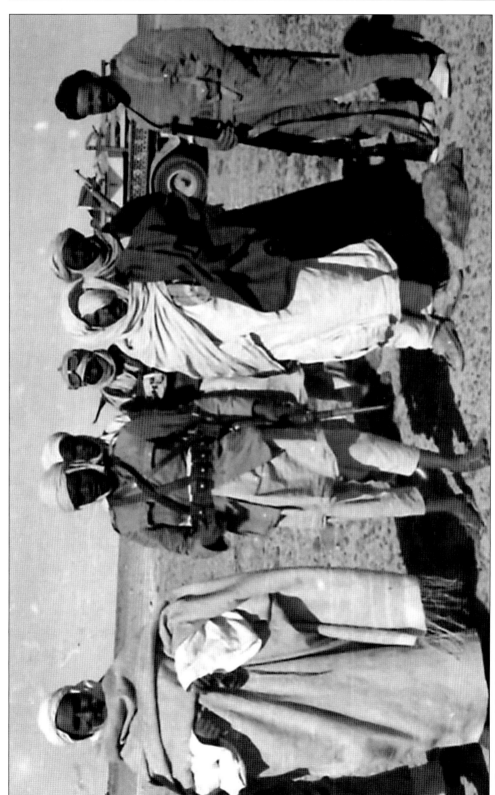

Patrolmen with locals and a patrol truck in the background. Note the commando style of the only visible patrolman. (Churchill Archives Centre, Ralph Bagnold, BGND, C12, Vol I, ID: E.49)

Four Chevrolet WB outside the fort in Kufra, closest to the camera is the R patrol signals vehicle "ROTOWHERO". Photo from March 1941. (Churchill Archives Centre, Ralph Bagnold, BGND, C12, Vol I, ID: DL 25-206)

A cup of tea before being evacuated from Kufra to Cairo by the LRDG "air force". A photo from September 1942. (Churchill Archives Centre, Ralph Bagnold, BGND, C12, Vol I, ID: E.53)

Chad under pressure is pushed up through the sandstone slabs in the lower parts of the desert. And where there is water there is life. Certainly, there was poverty in Kufra, but there are wonderful palm trees there, without which it would have been hopeless to settle on the spot. It's amazing what this wonderful tree can yield: dates to eat, palm wine to drink, material for buildings and fires, large evergreen leaves for roof tiles, carpets, baskets and ropes. And not least shadow for tired and sun scorched soldiers.[13]

Italy had also done some good things for Kufra, and this without taxing the local Senussi. The Italians had built a school, a small hospital, a mosque and housing. All these came to benefit the British staffs and units. The Senussi themselves preferred to live in their traditional clay buildings, which work very well as it virtually never rains in Kufra.

The defeat of Italy in eastern Libya, Cyrenaica, also meant that they evacuated their forces from the oases around Kufra. Taiserbo, Zighen, Rebiana and others thus fell into British hands without fighting. But with the exception of the Zighen, they were populated by tribes who, although peaceful, could be suspected of providing the enemy with information. The airfield at Taiserbo was important to ensure that no enemy aircraft could use it, but S Patrol did not have the time to check things out there, and left that task to R Patrol who took the airfield on April 9 1941.

Although LRDG was doing fine, that was not the case for the rest of the British Army. The Afrika Korps under General Erwin Rommel launched (March 28 1941) the offensive that, in record time, pushed the British out of Cyrenaica except for Tobruk, which was besieged, and Kufra, that was too distant. For LRDG, it was therefore even more important to establish itself in Kufra, and it was decided that the entire unit except G and Y Patrol would be based there.

Ralph Bagnold was promoted to Lieutenant Colonel and appointed commander of the combined British-French force in Kufra. In addition to this job, he would act as a kind of local governor and carry out tasks on behalf of the administrations in Egypt and Chad. To assist him, Bagnold was given two political officers and 30 Libyan policemen.[14] In case the Kufra base was forced to evacuate, he himself would have to organize this. There would be no assistance from either air or ground units.

On 9 April 1941 - the same day that Rommel's siege of Tobruk began – most of the LRDG left Cairo and headed towards Kufra in four columns. The B-column reached Kufra on 19 April 19, without mishaps, but unfortunately, things did not go as well for the A-column that traveled around Gilf Kebir along with Heavy Section, equipped with brand new White 10-ton trucks. A good part of the stretch the ground was fine, it felt almost like driving on a football field. But since the cars were heavily loaded, they encountered severe difficulties when they reached soft sand. Only after a great deal of sand shoveling, Kufra was finally reached on 25 April.

Bagnold immediately became aware of a major challenge: how could Kufra be provided with the amount of goods required by a real garrison? The petrol transports necessary for patrol missions alone was a huge problem. Plus transports of weapons and ammunition, food and replacements. The solution, it was believed, was in Sudan.[15] Now that the Italians were about to be defeated in Abyssinia (today Ethiopia), trucks from that theatre of operations could be released for the task of supplying Kufra. But it was no walk in the park. From the British base Wadi Halfa next to the Nile at the border between Sudan and Egypt to Kufra, it was 1,120 kilometres over roadless sand. First, 3-toners and 30-cwts were used, which were almost worn out and fitted with just standard road tires. The route was untested, the maps were poor and the native drivers had no experience of desert driving!

13   Lloyd Owen, pp. 38-39.
14   *Special Forces in the Desert War 1940-43*, p. 48-49.
15   Kennedy Shaw, p. 86; *Special Forces in the Desert War 1940-43*, p. 48-49.

Nevertheless, the first supply convoy of about a 100 trucks left Wadi Halfa on 28 April. Twenty cars totally broke down and the necessary spare parts were missing. After some 600 kilometers, the convoy was forced to stop and reorganize. In the middle of nowhere, the men had to unload and reload unto 30-cwts that drove in shuttle traffic to Kufra. The first part of the Sudan convoy thus arrived on 7 May, and the last part only on 13 May. In total, 70 tonnes of supplies were delivered. It was at the last minute. The LRDG's own supplies were just about finished. Had Kufra not been resupplied, all air and ground operations via Kufra, first of all the offensive ones, would have been impossible.[16]

LRDG Air Force

The RAF was at this stage not keen to assist the LRDG with any more airplanes and pilots. Part of the reason may have been the secrecy that surrounded the unit at the time, which meant that few understood what the LRDG was good for. Bill Kennedy Shaw described in his war memoirs how the LRDG then went about to create its own air arm:

> In January of 1941 Guy Prendergast had arrived from England to join the unit as second-in-command. He had great experience of desert travel, with Bagnold in the early days, in Egypt and Palestine, in Iraq and Iran […] In addition he had about a thousand flying hours to his credit as a private aircraft owner, many of them in Egypt and the Sudan. He saw at once how valuable aircraft would be to LRDG, based on Kufra and needing quick contact with GHQ in Cairo, and set about to make an air force of his own.
>
> At the beginning there were many difficulties. The RAF, perhaps naturally enough, were very sticky. They could not spare us men or machines and did not at all like the idea of an independent unit like LRDG having its own aircraft. Their view was that all military aeroplanes in the British Empire must be under RAF control, and for a time they refused to give us [identification] numbers or allow us to paint the roundels on the wings, without which we should have been shot down immediately. In the end they were only dislodged from this attitude by Very High Authority.[17]

Prendergast managed to get two aircraft, that were called Big Waco and Little Waco. He had bought them from Egyptian private owners. What about the Waco name? It was for the Weaver Aircraft Corporation of Ohio. Prendergast flew one and Sergeant Barker, a New Zealand pilot, the other.[18] There was simply no ground staff, the pilots themselves had to do the regular maintenance, an Egyptian aircraft company the bigger stuff.

About the effectiveness of this small unit Shaw wrote:

> The Wacos earned their keep over and over again — in visits to Middle East and Army Headquarters from Siwa, Kufra, Jalo and Hon; in bringing in wounded men and taking spare parts out to the patrols. And it says a lot for the skill of the pilots and navigators that there was never a disaster or anything approaching one.[19]

Spare parts for the Waco aircraft initially had to be ordered from the United States via London, which became a bit ridiculous.

---

16   *Special Forces in the Desert War 1940-43*, p. 68.
17   Kennedy Shaw, pp. 84-85.
18   *Special Forces in the Desert War 1940-43*, p. 76.
19   Kennedy Shaw, p. 86.

In the end, the RAF took over maintenance, but without confirming it in writing. Perhaps they were anxious not to be held responsible for the unauthorized "LRDG Air Force". The RAF did also later base three Westland Lysander liaison aircraft and three older Gloster Gladiator biplane fighters in Kufra. But they mostly stayed on the ground due to their non-desert characteristics. An additional plane, an outdated Bristol Bombay bomber, proved to be somewhat more useful, for transporting wounded.

New "business opportunities" on the coast

Mussolini´s forces were not particularly active in the desert between April and July 1941. The same was true for LRDG, except for First Lieutenant Jake Easonsmith, who almost single-handedly blew up a dozen enemy trucks.

The Italians were still licking their wounds after the defeat against Wavell's troops. The *Deutsches Afrikakorps* (DAK) under Rommel, however, had in a frighteningly quick move reached the Egyptian border, and held their ground there. His further advance was hindered by not least the Australian 9th Division, that was holding out in Tobruk and had repelled two DAK attacks. Rommel also knew that by capturing the port of Tobruk he would greatly reduce the length of his supply lines.

In general, in April 1941 the Allied generals in North Africa were busy re-grouping after their retreat from Cyrenaica, and planning for counterattacks around the Egypt-Libya border on the coast, to reach Tobruk.[20] Rommel, with his successful offensive, had a new problem, a particularly extended supply line along the coast from Tripoli and Benghazi to Sollum on the Egyptian border. Here, there were new "business opportunities" for LRDG.

20   *Special Forces in the Desert War 1940-43*, p. 47.

7

Road-watching and bluffing

From April 1941 most of LRDG had been in Kufra with Bagnold as both local commander and governor. The Allied offensive of 15-27 May supposed to save Tobruk failed both to free the town and cause any significant losses on the German side. In fact, the opposite happened, as in addition to repairing their own tanks, the German salvage teams were able to seize also several disabled British tanks, patch them up and send them off against their erstwhile owners.

With the British back on the other side of the Egyptian border, General Erwin Rommel could carefully consolidate his positions. He thus ordered more mine fields, well covered by eighty-eights, those 8.8 cm anti-aircraft guns that Rommel during the conquest of France so successfully used against enemy armour. Now he could calmly wait for the next British attack. But maybe not so calmly. For both in the back and in the side, German and Italian supply convoys experienced unpleasant contacts with small patrols that quickly disappeared into the desert while Axis trucks exploded behind them and horrified crews ran in all directions. They were the victims of direct action by the Ghost Patrol (There were at all times several patrols in the LRDG, but the Italian name for the LRDG was in the singular form).

The German and Italian supply lines had been stretched out to nearly 1,500 kilometres, from Tripoli to Sollum, and attacking them ought to force Rommel to detach some frontline units for road protection. Meaning less units for the siege of Tobruk and the positions at the Egyptian border.

At this point in the Second World War, London was worried that Hitler's attack on the Soviet Union might be successful. The worst case scenario in the heads of the Middle East Command generals was that German success against the Soviets would entail German attacks against Egypt also through Turkey and Syria. In addition to many regular units, defending against such attacks also required patrols that could perform raids or long range reconnaissance work in that direction. So, the War Office had finally realized the merits of the LRDG concept, and as a consequence, Ralph Bagnold was made a colonel and assigned to the special section of GHQ in Cairo. There he would set up new patrols while coordinating the growing number of special forces. The job of commanding LRDG was taken over by Lieutenant Colonel Guy Prendergast, at least as low-key as Bagnold, but also very knowledgeable about the demands and opportunities of desert warfare.[1]

Unlike Bagnold, Prendergast was, as previously mentioned, a trained pilot, which was very useful in his new role. Flying a Waco-plane, he could maintain personal and quick contact with his desert patrols and also the top brass in Cairo, not least Bagnold.

In late September 1941, the Western Desert Force was reorganized into the new and soon legendary formation, the 8th Army, and on 1 October, LRDG was assigned to this army. A new army headquarters was established on 24 September in Ma'aten Bagush near the Libyan border, 365 kilometres west of Cairo. Thanks to the fact that Bagnold was placed in the decision making

---

1   *Special Forces in the Desert War 1940-43*, pp. 68-69.

centre, he was able to participate in discussions about the LRDG's role in Operation Crusader. He could therefore directly affect decisions about the Ghost Patrol in the coming attack.[2]

The most important task of all was now to secure credible information about enemy troop movements, to make it possible to interpret the enemy's reactions to the British offensive.[3] It was absolutely essential that the patrolmen quickly could send tactical information. In fact, if they discovered something extra important just before or during the operation, they were allowed to send the information in plain text. Since radio communication was usually broadcast in cipher, this was exceptional, and a sign of the increased importance given to the time factor.

The modern German way of waging war had penetrated conservative British military thinking. Orders went faster with the Germans, and low-level initiative was actually more encouraged on the German side – i.e. contrary to the perception that Germans just clicked their heels and only followed orders. However, from the Italians there was not much to learn, even though their warfighting skills had improved a bit since Wavell's offensive at the beginning of the year.

Bearded warriors

LRDG men came from some fifty different units and from many parts of the British Empire, which meant some rather motley patrols. This, in combination with week after week without being able to wash resulted in an unusual appearance. Those who originally came from one of the Guards regiments often made an effort even out in the desert to look smart, but generally speaking soon all patrolmen looked pretty wild and their beards were the longest in the British Army. In fact, Sir Cecil Beaton, then a war correspondent visiting the Siwa Oasis, was somewhat shocked by a group of patrolmen who had just returned from a mission and described them with few flattering words, even stating that one of them "…with ginger matting for hair, and red eyes staring from a blue-grey dusty face, looked no more human than an ape".[4] In spite of the water shortage and the beards, patrolmen still tried to maintain some personal hygiene. Luckily, in the desert the sand is extremely clean. Sir Beaton, who later gained royal fame, kept a special affection for the LRDG.

The coastal road watch

If LRDG would be able to continuously observe and record enemy traffic on Libya's only decent road – the coastal road, then many valuable insights could be gained.[5] But what about the RAF, could not pilots provide photos of the road convoys? Well, in contrast to aerial reconnaissance, surveillance from the ground was both unaffected by the weather and night – at night the patrolmen would move closer to the road. It also became apparent that the level of detail they provided, e.g. of unit markings painted on vehicles, could never be matched by RAF photographs.

Initially, S Patrol was given this task and started its journey to the coast from the oasis of Zighen northwest of Kufra on 15 September 1941 with Second Lieutenant John Olivey as the patrol commander and Second Lieutenant Tony Browne as patrol navigator and intelligence officer. They

2   Morgan, p. 46.
3   *Special Forces in the Desert War 1940-43*, p. 79.
4   Cecil Beaton & Richard Buckle, *Self portrait with friends: the selected diaries of Cecil Beaton, 1926-1974* (New York: The New York Times Book Company, 1982), p. 98.
5   *Special Forces in the Desert War 1940-43*, p. 79.

German armour passing through the Italian *Arco dei Fileni*, which to LRDG patrolmen became "Marble Arch". This was one of Mussolini´s largest monuments in Africa, marking the border between Libya´s two northern regions Tripolitania and Cyrenaica. (Deutsches Bundesarchiv)

LRDG in the same place as the German Panzers, i.e. by "Marble Arch". (LRDG Preservation Society)

travelled in four 30-cwt trucks and one 15-cwt command car. The purpose was to spy on the traffic along the coastal road west of El Agheila, and to be able to do this over a longer period of time they were to establish an observation post there. Cairo had a list of stuff they wanted to know: the number and type of armored vehicles, the number of artillery pieces and trucks, whether the convoys constituted combat units or supply services, types and numbers of escort vehicles in supply convoys and at where in the convoys the escorts were.[6]

The patrol's order was to unnoticeably establish itself on the coast in an area completely controlled by Rommel, preferably close to Ras Umm el Garanig. Offensive actions by the patrol were strictly forbidden. In case of an enemy attack, Olivey would decide if the spying would continue or if the patrol should interrupt and return with the information that had been obtained. Better than no information at all.

It was vital that nothing leaked to the Axis forces about the road watchers and their positions. It's quite amazing that they were able to carry on for so long, because some locals did become aware of the LRDG observation teams. Still, they were never betrayed and the reason was the brutality the Italians had shown towards the local population. The locals above all wanted to be rid of the Italians. After that, also the Brits and the Germans.

To be able to observe an enemy road over a long period of time, extreme security measures were necessary. Everyone in the patrol was carefully instructed to always bring home or very properly bury all cans, papers, cigarette packages and other things that most people usually chuck away without thinking. If the enemy discovered even the most insignificant item with English text, he would understand that British troops were in the area.

Patrol commander Olivey chose a good viewing point and the men took turns observing the road, day and night, noting everything that appeared. At the end of an observation period a protocol was drawn up that summarized things. Here is a typical flash from the road watch:

- Trucks 3-10 tonnes   eastbound 1 218   westbound 764
- Military and civilian cars eastbound 131   westbound 59
- Motorcycles   eastbound 111   westbound 13

Night traffic was sparse, after 22.30 it often stopped. Traffic was busiest between sunrise and 10.30, and between 16:00 and sunset. There was never much traffic at night but at dusk the two men on duty would move down closer to the road and judge by the sound the types of passing vehicles. The traffic was mainly in the form of convoys, and most appeared to be of a supply character, not combat troops.[7]

Back in camp the rest of the patrol would have an alert sentry while some men slept, some read or played bridge. After dark the wireless masts in the camp would go up and especially if enemy tanks had gone by this information, forwarded by Group HQ in Siwa and later Kufra, was soon de-coded in Cairo and very soon formed an essential part of a briefing.

On two occasions, convoys stayed and slept close to the observers, uncomfortably close because even a small movement could be noticed in the desert night. The last day of S Patrol´s first road watch two German field police posts were set up quite close, and the traffic increased so much it was almost like Piccadilly Circus, despite being in a desert landscape recently frequented mainly by camels.

6   Lloyd Owen, p. 49.
7   Kennedy Shaw, p. 210.

After four days, S Patrol returned to Zighen without problems. It had been an educational excursion.[8]

Professional tankspotters

The coastal road observations conducted for the Allied top brass in Cairo turned into one of the LRDG's most valued contributions to the war effort. A more permanent observation post was therefore established near "Marble Arch" on the border between the Libyan provinces of Cyrenaica and Tripolitania. "Marble Arch" was the name that Allied soldiers used for the 31 metre tall Italian monument erected by Marshal Balbo close to Ra's Lanuf. This solid piece of Italian megalomania gave Allied troops an excellent orientation point in the landscape.

The area was sparsely populated, which reduced the risk of discovery. Risk-free it was not, the closer you came to Tripoli, the greater the risk of meeting hostile locals.[9]

The coastal road watch became a major business for the LRDG and went on most intensely between March and December 1942. During that time not a single enemy vehicle and not a single piece of artillery passed unnoticed from Tripoli via the battlefields in Cyrenaica to the east. The traffic westwards was of course also noted, and the increasing traffic in that direction in late 1942 confirmed the size and seriousness of Rommel's retreat. Towards the end of this very long observation assignment, the location of the road watch had to be moved west to register the last part of the retreat.

The actual surveillance work was mostly conducted about 200 metres from the road. But during the night the two observers on duty were closer to the road, often just 30 metres. The main part of the patrol was hidden a few kilometres from the observers. A patrol served as "tankspotters" for seven to ten days in a row, then it was replaced. Because it took about four days to get to the place from Siwa or Kufra, the coastal road watch job involved a total of three patrols; one on the job, one going out and one returning.

To help the patrolmen get better at identifying tanks, guns, uniforms and unit markings, the ambitious Captain Enoch Powell used to fly from HQ in Cairo to Siwa and hold lessons about Axis forces and their equipment.[10] He would always bring an album with fresh photographs and drawings that focused on key features such as muzzle brakes and road wheels on tanks. At this time of the war, the Royal Navy and RAF were sinking half of Rommel's supplies. Seemingly insignificant details from the patrolmen could confirm the effect of their operations against Axis logistics. Enoch Powell would later become a member of parliament and minister for health.

Although it entailed risking the long term reconnaissance mission of the LRDG, impatient staff officers sometimes called for the patrols on the coastal road to also "harass" the enemy. But raids, ambushes or sabotage often triggered a large search for the culprits. A major search of the road watch area was not on the wish list of the LRDG. However, one can understand that direct action against the enemy was tempting, because from late 1941 desert patrol raids, boosted by the entry of the SAS, proved to be a very profitable venture. But before we look at how the LRDG-SAS partnership started, let us leave the North African coast and go back deep into the desert, about three hundred kilometres inland, to an LRDG operation about planting deliberately false information, i.e. disinformation.

8   Kennedy Shaw, p. 233.
9   Kennedy Shaw, p. 151; *Special Forces in the Desert War 1940-43*, p. 80.
10   Sadler, p. 74.

Desert bluffers

Before Operation Crusader was launched to relieve the Siege of Tobruk, the LRDG was ordered to somehow plant a fake map near Jalo to make the enemy believe that a huge British force would attack Jalo from the east. The map had very "credible" notes scribbled on it, like some words about the nature of the terrain and distance calculations.

The patrol for this "bluffing mission" was assembled by Bill Kennedy Shaw, and he made Second Lieutenant "Tony" Browne patrol commander, who chose 10 men to go with him. They traveled from Kufra via Zighen in three 30-cwt Fords, and arrived on 9 November 1941 at a point next to the northern edge of the Jikerra oasis, 30 kilometres east of Jalo. Having safely arrived, they noted a Bedouin riding on a camel, and because it was obvious that the Bedouin was on his way to the water well of El Aseila, they steered their vehicles towards that well. When the patrolmen arrived they made a fire and had a small meal. After a while, the Bedouin also arrived, but watched from a distance. He obviously was not keen to talk with the patrolmen, which was a good sign. The patrol had arranged some items on the ground, and all of a sudden acted as if they were in a great hurry, "accidentally" leaving behind a map board, scale and protractor.

A fortnight later Brigadier Denys Reid marched on Jalo with a British, Indian and South African brigade, guided by the LRDG. This force took the oasis of Aujila one afternoon, made a skillful night march to the outskirts of Jalo, and attacked the next day. Kennedy Shaw later remarked about the scene that followed:

> By evening the defence had crumbled and Reid jumped into his car, drove up to the gate of the fort and found the seventy Italian officers of the garrison sitting calmly down to dinner. They soon made it plain to him that they regarded the tiresome business of fighting as being happily disposed of.[11]

When the victors entered the Italian commander's office in Jalo they found a large map including details that had no doubt been copied from the map left by the well. The "plant" had been successful.[12]

---

11   Kennedy Shaw, pp. 122-123.
12   *Special Forces in the Desert War 1940-43*, p. 92.

8

LRDG during Operation Crusader

British intelligence analysts using data provided by the LRDG indicated that Rommel's preparations for an attack against Tobruk would be almost complete by the third week of November 1941.[1] But it was also sensitive situation for Rommel, at this late point he could regroup for defense only with great difficulty. In other words, it was a good moment for the Allies to strike against the Axis forces in Libya. Although not yet keen to strike, the generals in Cairo were under intense pressure from London to start an offensive. In their desperation, the generals decided to bolster the conventional attack with two high-risk raids, one airborne against the Luftwaffe and one amphibious special operation directly against Rommel's HQ.

LRDG was in the context of Operation Crusader mainly a force for observing enemy movements along the desert routes around Bir Hacheim, El Adem, Mechili and Bir Tengeder, as well as along the old caravan trail Trigh el Abd. The patrols were also to keep an eye on the northern approach to the Jalo Oasis, recently taken with ease from the Italians. If Rommel were to take over Jalo and position units there, they could quickly grow into a threat to the British left flank.

However, two LRDG patrols had received very different orders. Let us first look at R1 Patrol under the command of Lieutenant Jake Easonsmith. This patrol was to pick up some paratroopers led by a long Scottish captain called David Stirling from something called L Detachment, Special Air Service Brigade. Stirling was from an ancient family but had dropped out of Cambridge, then tried and failed to become an artist in Paris. At the Scots Guards regimental depot he had been described by his instructors as an "irresponsible and unremarkable soldier". For a while, Stirling had been on his way to Finland to assist that country during Stalin's Winter War, but the mission to Finland never materialized. Stirling's "brigade" was also not that impressive; it consisted of not even a hundred men. "L Detachment, Special Air Service Brigade" was a name created to scare the Germans once they got wind of the unit's existence.

Helping some "parashots"

The mission of Stirling's "parashots", as the patrolmen first called them, was to land by parachute on 16 November and destroy as many aircraft as possible on the five airfields near Gazala and Tmimi, thus weakening German air power on the eve of Operation Crusader. The SAS men were then to find the LRDG vehicles that would bring them to the Siwa Oasis. This was no minor experiment as it would be the first operational parachute operation in the Middle East theatre, plus the first SAS raid ever.[2]

The chosen day came with flashes of lightning and unusually strong winds.[3] But David Stirling felt pressure from so many sides, that he found it impossible to postpone the mission. As a result

---

1   *Special Forces in the Desert War 1940-43*, p. 93.
2   *Special Forces in the Desert War 1940-43*, p. 94; Morgan, p. 24; Mortimer (2015:1), p. 100.
3   James D. Ladd, *SAS Operations* (London: Robert Hale, 1986), pp. 1-3; Mortimer (2015:1), p. 114.

of the terrible weather the RAF dropped the "parashots" wide of their target and when they had landed, wind, rain and mud hindered them still more. The only SAS team to reach their target was killed. Of the 64 men in the first SAS operation, only 22 came back. The remainder were all killed or captured. The deeply shocked SAS men were brought back by the LRDG. It is quite surprising that neither did David Stirling then give up his SAS project, nor was the SAS disbanded.[4]

The disaster of its first raid meant an end to SAS airborne operations in Africa, but not the end of the unit itself. Equally remarkable is that the LRDG volunteered to replace the method of parachuting to the target area. How this offer was made has been told by David Lloyd Owen, the LRDG officer who was there with David Stirling, just after the disaster:

> We sat down and had a mug of tea together while he told me the story of his heartbreaking failure and how from the start very little had gone right. But, of course, Stirling was not in any way downhearted; he was even then turning over in his mind all the mistakes that had been made and the lessons that he could learn from his first abortive attempt. He was so certain that he could succeed and nothing was going to stop him - if he was given another chance. What a man! Failure meant nothing more to him than to generate fierce determination to be successful next time. [...]
>
> While he was telling me of the events of the last few days, and of his ideas for the future, I detected in him just the slightest doubt that parachuting was really the answer to getting to his objective without fail. There were always, he told me, the limitations imposed by weather conditions quite apart from the problem of availability of aircraft. At that stage of the war the techniques of accurate dropping were certainly far from developed for either bombs or bodies, and there was no guarantee that anyone would be landed exactly as planned, even on the brightest of moonlit nights.
>
> Suddenly an idea came to me. Surely the answer was for the LRDG to convey the SAS parties to within a few miles of their targets? We would then lie off while they were doing whatever they had in mind, and we could return a day or so later to collect them.[5]

This was one of the best ideas Stirling would ever hear, and some weeks later he would put the idea into action.

Against Rommel's HQ

Whereas the SAS men at the time were basically paratroopers and saboteurs, there were also some more classic spies in need of a desert taxi. T2 Patrol led by Captain Anthony Hunter and Second Lieutenant Paul Freyberg - General Freyberg's son – received the task of bringing Intelligence Corps/ SOE Captain John Haselden and some of his pro-Allied Arabs to an area not far from Rommel's own HQ. After that, the patrol would go into hiding and stay hidden until it received a code word from Cairo meaning it should start a road watch between Mechili and Benghazi. Then, just before returning to Siwa, the patrol was to pick up Haselden and his men. That was the idea.

In prewar Egypt there lived a number of British teachers and businessmen with Arabic contacts and special language skills. One of them was Captain John Haselden. He was born in Ramlah outside Alexandria and was a cotton broker before the war. He had the perfect looks for a spy in North Africa, as his mother was Italian, and his Arabic was so perfect that he could be taken for

4   Thompson, p. 55.
5   Lloyd Owen, pp. 60-61.

an Arab, even by Arabs. In fact, he spoke several Arabic dialects. This is how Bill Kennedy-Shaw described John Haselden:

> Haselden was the outstanding personality of the dozen odd men who worked with the tribes in Cyrenaica behind the Axis lines. Untiring, strong, courageous, never without some new scheme for outwitting the enemy, yet with a slow and easy-going way of setting about a job which was far more successful with the Arabs than the usual European insistence on precision and punctuality which they neither like nor understand.[6]

At the time he started to cooperate with the LRDG, Haselden was an officer of the Libyan Arab Force and specialized in commando operations, and was also tasked with connecting with the Arab population in occupied territories.[7] Of course, his job also included listening to rumours among the locals.

When T2 Patrol with Haselden and the Arabs reached the old camel trail Trigh el Abd (the most important alternative to the coastal road) there were clear signs that it had been recently used. The aerial activity above was lively and consisted mainly of German planes traveling east-west. Although several of them flew at only about 900 meters, nobody seemed to notice T2 Patrol. There was a problem getting good bearings and thus navigating in this landscape, but thanks to John Haselden and one of the Arabs, they reached Wadi el Heleighima, a deep gorge over which a bridge leads to the Benghazi road.

Shelter was found in a wadi a few kilometres from the road and during the night Haselden left the patrol together with one of the Arabs to execute their part in Operation Flipper. The operation included among its objectives an attack on the headquarters of Erwin Rommel at Beda Littoria. It was timed for the night of 17/18 November 1941, just before the start of Operation Crusader.[8] Although not specified in the orders, the goal of the raid was to kill or capture Rommel, and thus thoroughly disrupt all German units before the start of Crusader. Rommel's headquarters was believed to be at Beda Littoria, because Captain John Haselden had previously reconnoitered the area disguised as an Arab and reported that Rommel's own car came and went from the former Prefecture.

On 10 November, two Royal Navy submarines carried a group of commandos from Alexandria. The men were mainly from No. 11 (Scottish) Commando.[9] On the night of 14/15 November 1941, one group of them landed on the beach of Khashm al-Kalb, guided by Special Boat Section (SBS) teams in folding canoes. Once ashore, they made contact with Haselden. The weather deteriorated and the next group had a much more difficult time getting ashore. Remember David Stirling's severe weather problems?

With only 34 of the 59 men needed and after a 29 km night march in torrential rain, the German HQ was attacked. Four Germans were killed, none of them Rommel. A fuel depot was destroyed. Not exactly what the raiders had hoped they would accomplish, and only three of them were able to get away, two were killed and 28 of them were captured. Unbeknownst to the planners of Operation Flipper, Beda Littoria had only briefly been Rommel's HQ and had been taken over by his chief quartermaster. Some weeks earlier, Rommel had moved his headquarters nearer to Tobruk. He wanted to be closer to the action. However, right then, during the raid, he was enjoying some leave in Rome, staying at the Hotel Eden with his wife Lucie.

6   Kennedy Shaw, p. 119.
7   Michael Asher, *Get Rommel* (London: Cassell, 2005), p. 103.
8   Kennedy Shaw, p. 119.
9   Asher, p. 164.

Nevertheless, John Haselden had done his best for the operation and for his part in it he was awarded a bar to his Military Cross, which was much later announced in the *London Gazette*. The recommendation read:

Captain Haselden was dropped by the Long Range Desert Group in the area of Slonta prior to the raid carried out by a detachment of the Middle East Commandos on General Rommel's HQ at Sidi Rafa. Capt. Haselden was dressed in British battle dress but wearing a djard and Arab head-dress walked a distance of nearly 100 miles through the heart of the enemy territory in order to make certain reconnaissances prior to the landing of the detachment. After ascertaining the situation regarding enemy and friendly Arab forces in the area he made his way to the selected beach and there awaited our landing which he guided in by pre-arranged signals. Having passed on vital information about the enemy which was immediately transmitted to the Royal Navy to Cairo and having explained the situation ashore to our raiding party and guided us towards our objective, Capt. Haselden again made his way through miles of enemy territory to his appointed rendezvous with the Long Range Desert Group. On his journey back he succeeded in disrupting vital enemy communication […].[10]

Returning Haselden was not that easy for T2. Italian soldiers suddenly showed up in two trucks and opened fire on them with Breda guns. Hunter managed to shout so that the crew of his Bofors armed 30-cwt could retreat and warn the other troops. Then Hunter got lost and Freyberg had to take over, who managed to establish radio contact with Siwa HQ, which, after hearing his report, ordered the patrol to return immediately to Siwa. Since it was no longer possible for them to pick up John Haselden's group, HQ ordered another patrol to the area to try to pick up John Haselden and his Arabs. This rescue was seriously delayed by a combination of severe terrain and mechanical failures. Only on 1 December it was possible to bring Haselden and his men back. But there was a bonus, as the previously lost Captain Hunter had also made it to the rendezvous.[11]

What about the big picture? Before dawn on 18 November, Eighth Army under General Cunningham launched Operation Crusader, advancing west from its base at Mersa Matruh. Initially a lot went well for the tanks and infantry involved, not least thanks to some heavy rain just before the operation. The rain had grounded the Luftwaffe and thus the Allies had a fair element of surprise and could concentrate on looking for enemy tanks. By the end of the day, the 7th Armoured Brigade had reached Gabr Seleh, half way to Tobruk, without running into significant enemy forces.

Looking back both at the SAS and commando operations that were supposed to support Operation Crusader it is clear how much the weather factor was underestimated and also affected the operations, but also how the LRDG in both cases was able to save the surviving raiders.

Under friendly fire

For T2 Patrol, it was a happy end when the lost Captain Hunter returned, but some LRDG missions ended more badly. Y1 Patrol under Captain Frank Simms was on its way to Garet Meriem, about a hundred kilometres south of Tobruk. Before arriving they were attacked by three RAF planes whose crews were completely blind to the patrol's frantic signaling. To be shot at by your own side happens more often than most people imagine. War correspondents during the Second World War,

10   *London Gazette* (18 February 1943).
11   *Special Forces in the Desert War 1940-43*, p. 97.

and not only that war, rarely put such things in their reports, as it would it would not strengthen the home front.

The RAF planes hit Y1 Patrol's only radio car and it began to burn. Fortunately, the fire could be extinguished and the Y1 boys could get in touch with Y2 Patrol. A truck was detached to return to Siwa to quickly pick up a new radio car. When Y1 Patrol arrived in the area it was supposed to make observations in, it happened to find an unguarded German vehicle depot, about 30 trucks of different kinds. The patrolmen immediately started sabotaging them, with no lack of enthusiasm. However, during this mission, Lance-Corpral "Lofty" Carr went missing, and he did not appear at the agreed rendezvous site.

Carr later explained he had lost contact with his patrol on December 2 and then decided to walk to the area on the coastal road chosen as the starting point for the next raid.[12] He had both a map and a compass on him, and had memorized the upcoming mission and terrain. In the evening of 3 December he had discovered a Senussi camp where he received both shelter and food for a fortnight while fighting was raging nearby.

On 17 December British troops reached the camp and together with a wounded RAF officer also protected by the Senussi he was handed over to the Royal Artillery. He was back in Siwa just in time for Christmas. In fact, Lofty Carr is still alive at the time of writing (2018).

Smoking with the enemy

Although counting or killing Germans became the main focus after Rommel made his appearance, the Italians were still quite often on the LRDG agenda in late 1941. Sometimes fighting against them could be just surreal, as Captain David Lloyd Owen and his Y2 patrol experienced. It all began when the patrol by chance came upon a Ford containing three Italian and two Libyan soldiers. They were quickly captured and interrogated on the spot. One of the Italians stated they had been on their way to a fort close by. Lloyd Owen saw an opportunity and decided to investigate the matter quickly:

> Soon we could see this small desert outpost of the Italian Empire and I hoped that by driving straight up to it we could get reasonably near before the garrison suspected anything. As we approached I could see a man on the roof watching us through his glasses. Our Italian friend said they would probably surrender if we showed fight and so I decided to attack. We made a hasty plan, but I was not well versed in the art of attacking forts in unarmoured 30-cwt trucks.
>
> We drove forward in open formation till they began to fire by which time we were only about two hundred yards away and it was unwise to endanger the trucks further. So we left the drivers to guard the prisoners and rushed towards the fort on foot. We reached some outhouses unhurt and took cover.
>
> Then there ensued a short period of close range sniping during which we killed two of the enemy and made the others, keep their heads down. It seemed that we should have to change our plan of attack for I could see no end to this friendly sniping; it had done us no harm, but we numbered only eight and could hardly hope to take the place by storm. An idea came to me, a hope that we might bluff them into surrender. I shouted for the Italian prisoner who crawled up to me amidst a volley of shots from his friends. He came on, bravely and sat down with me behind a wall. I told him that I intended to offer the garrison

an armistice so that they could come out and discuss terms of surrender because I had strong reinforcements which would be arriving at any moment. I stood him up and with courage unusual in an Italian he walked towards the fort.

For some strange reason he seemed to regard himself on our side for he cajoled and implored the commander until he came out to meet me. The armistice had begun and I could not but laugh at this strange form of warfare as we shook hands and smoked cigarettes together. We talked for about 10 minutes but the commander was quite adamant that he would continue to fight. I said I was sorry as I had wished to avoid more bloodshed, wondering all the time what to do next in order to avoid an ignominious retreat. We shook hands once again and I gave him time to get back to his position before the battle was restarted.

We had done all we could with rifles, pistols and machineguns and the only trump card left to us was a grenade from a discharger cup. We didn't really know how to use the thing but hoped that a well-planted shot on the tower might silence opposition from that direction. I decided to renew the attack, firing everything at once and trying to get the range with the grenade thrower. With the good fortune that comes to beginners the first grenade landed full on the tower. Such a chance was too good to miss and we rushed headlong towards the fort, shouting savage cries and firing wildly at everything. This was too much for one Yeoman, left as horseholder with the trucks, and with a shout to his Italian prisoner, 'Here, look after this car,' he sped after us to join the fun. Before we had reached the walls we were met by the garrison, seventeen strong, pouring out of the gate with their hands held high.[13]

As so often in combat behind enemy lines, the disposal of the prisoners turned out to be a problem, for Lloyd Owen was still on his way to his main objective, the coast road. Finally, the Italians were dumped thirty miles south in the desert, given food and water and the general direction for a march to the closest village.

At the beginning of December 1941, Operation Crusader had been going on for many days, and both sides had delivered and received several punches. At Sidi Rezegh, the German 15th Panzer Division had erased a whole South African infantry brigade. But Rommel's Panzers were also badly worn and their numbers were going down. His siege forces around Tobruk were also under severe pressure.

On the British side, the Eighth Army commanding general Alan Cunningham had been fired. The commander of the entire Middle East Command, General Sir Claude Auchinleck, personally took over. Auchinleck gave clear orders and demanded reinforcements.

At the same time, Rommel's closest superiors in *Comando Supremo*, the Italian high command, announced that new supplies could not be expected before the end of December. Possibly, it could then be flown in from Sicily. "Flown in" meant that zero new tanks could be expected before the new year.

No place to hide

During operation Crusader the two patrols recruited from British Guards units, G1 and G2, had close contact with *Regia Aeronautica*, the Italian Air Force. G2 under First Lieutenant Alastair Timpson left Siwa on 15 November for his first combat assignment as an officer. Timpson came

13   Kennedy Shaw, pp. 115-116.

from the Scots Guards and was one of many young men thrown into the war directly from the school bench.

G2 reached Maaten El Grara in record time and could explore the area undisturbed until 18 November. Then, as they were gathering topographic information, an Italian *Sparviero* appeared over them and showed a lot of interest, going down real low, circling several times. There was just nowhere to hide for G2, but the Italians were also not sure of whose trucks they were. G2 decided to behave like a band of young fascists, making Roman salutes, laughing and waving to the plane in a most friendly manner. The acting was good, the real fascists up in the plane never pressed the firing button.

Since the patrols traveled for weeks on end in landscapes that had few if any places to hide, enemy flights were the greatest danger. It was no coincidence that LRDG was the champion of erecting camouflage nets. At the same time, it was dangerous for the aircraft to underestimate the weapons onboard the trucks, especially after the LRDG began to get those ex-RAF guns and the Italian Bredas.[14]

Three days after the G2's contact with *Regia Aeronautica* it was time again for an encounter. G2 was in hiding near Ma'aten Grara, watching for cross-desert traffic from Agedabia to Tobruk, when a Fiat BR.20 medium bomber, with one engine spluttering, came low over the cars and force-landed behind a rise. When Timpson arrived on the scene, the Italians were busy putting up their aerial to signal for help. They might have gotten it from G2 if the rear-gunner, still inside the aircraft, had not jumped so hurriedly to his gun. Several G2 trucks opened up against the sitting duck. After the brief battle G2 sent two prisoners back to Siwa, the rest of the crew were buried beside the ashes of their plane.

A Chevrolet with sand mats and sand channels clearly visible. (Churchill Archives Centre, Ralph Bagnold, BGND, C12, Vol I, ID: E.53)

14   Lloyd Owen, p. 81.

9

With the SAS again

On 27 November 1941, the situation for the Allies was critical. Operation Crusader had started well for the Allies, and then gone bad. News of the South African brigade's defeat at Sidi Rezegh affected all Allied units in North Africa. 8th Army headquarters came up with several ideas in order to rescue Operation Crusader, which resulted in the LRDG turning from reconnaissance to focus more on direct action.

West of the Great Sand Sea and south of Sirte Bay lies the previously mentioned Jalo Oasis. It is about 19 kilometres long and 11 kilometres in the widest place. With its size and strategic location far out in the desert combined with good access to water, this oasis was important for both sides. That's why the British wanted to secure Jalo so badly, which they succeeded in doing on 24 November. From early December three LRDG patrols were based in Jalo: S1 under Captain Charles Holliman, S2 under Lieutenant John Olivey and T2 under Lieutenant "Bing" Morris. There was also the heavy weapons section under the Second Lieutenant "Blitz" Eitzen, with LRDG's heaviest gun, a 25-pounder field gun and howitzer.[1]

On 8 December, S1 Patrol, comprising 19 Rhodesian soldiers, left Jalo Oasis with two SAS raiding parties aboard their seven Chevrolet trucks. David Stirling led one of the teams, the other his second-in-command, an Ulster-born lawyer and rugby player, Lieutenant "Paddy" Mayne. The destination was the airfields at Sirte and Tamet, some 560 kilometres to the northwest.[2]

Paddy Mayne and his eight men had been longing for a "beat-up", meaning a raid, ever since the great parachute disaster. At Tamet they got their opportunity. Mayne kicked open the door of a small house by the airfield, to find himself standing in front of a number of German and Italian aircrew who had just been resting and having a good time. At first the two sides had just stared at each other, the Axis fliers obviously hardly believing their eyes. When a young German airman arose and moved backwards, Mayne fired his Colt 45. The airmen then found their sidearms and started shooting back. While four of Mayne's team stayed to shoot it out with the airmen, Mayne and four others moved on, planting Lewes bombs in a petrol depot and all the aircraft that they could find in the dark.

An archetypal cockney soldier by the name of Bob Bennett was there with Paddy Mayne and later recounted the action that followed thus:

> We got moving fast, but even so the first bomb went off before we even cleared the airfield. We had to stop to look, didn't we. What a sight, flames and muck all over the place. We headed straight out to the LRDG lads. There was a bit of a kerfuffle when the Krauts caught us using flashing lights to find the RV [rendezvous], they started flashing their own but we used our whistles as a back-up and we got back OK.

---

1   Jenner & List, p. 14.
2   Ladd, p. 19.

Paddy Mayne and his team had destroyed an amazing number of aircraft, possibly as many as 24. In addition they had killed an unknown number of Axis airmen. Amazingly, everyone in Mayne's team made it back alive and were able to return to Tamet airfield less than two weeks later, laying waste to 27 planes that had replaced the ones they had recently destroyed.[3] Mayne was to blow up yet more aircraft, beating the score of most Allied ace pilots. In fact, at least once, after having run out of small bombs, he had used his considerable strength to disable an aircraft, he was able to rip out an instrument panel.

Even better "beat-ups"

More spectacular LRDG-based SAS "beat-ups" followed. On 21 December S2 Patrol delivered a five-man SAS team led by Lieutenant Bill Fraser close to the Agedabia airfield. They were extremely lucky, as they twice tripped over tripwires that did not result in any alarm or explosion of any kind. Detours were necessary to avoid sentries and gun positions. They reached the first aircraft just after midnight 22 December and were able to unhindered lay charges in no less than 37 aircraft and one depot.

While Fraser's team withdrew from Agedabia airfield they experienced the immense satisfaction of hearing at least 40 explosions and then they both heard and felt a massive roar that must have been a whole bomb depot going off. Again, not a single SAS trooper was killed, or even hurt. However, while going back to base their comrades in S2 Patrol suffered two killed from air attack. There was some extra tragedy in this because Laurence Ashby and Robert Riggs were not killed by an Axis fighter but by the RAF. In other words another case of "friendly fire" that would only be reported to the public long after the war.

During this period, from trial and error, the SAS and LRDG began to realize that the ideal method of destroying parked aircraft was to drive the vehicles between the rows of aircraft, and then engage mainly by machine gun fire and hand grenades.

What about the German view of these raids? While some aircraft reported to have been destroyed nevertheless were possible to repair (still meaning they were not operational for a long period of time) it is interesting to note the following words about the LRDG in a German intelligence summary:

> The LRDG plays an extremely important part in the enemy sabotage organization. The selection and training of the men, the strength, speed and camouflage of the vehicles for the country in which they have to operate have enabled the Group to carry out very effective work, particularly in the destruction of aircraft on the landing grounds at Agedabia and Tamet.[4]

The Kiwi T2 Patrol commanded by Lieutenant "Bing" Morris took part in a Hollywood-style raid as a consequence of the LRDG-SAS raiding partnership. It all started with T2 picking up a dozen SAS men on 10 December. The twin objectives were the El Agheila landing-ground, and an anchorage at nearby Mersa Brega used to unload Axis supplies. However, the raiders found that the landing-ground was then not being used. The other objective, the anchorage, remained. Morris then established that any cross-country approach to it was impossible due to nasty salt marshes. So

---

3   Gavin Mortimer, *Stirling's Desert Triumph* (Oxford: Osprey, 2015:2), p. 20.
4   John W. Gordon, *The Other Desert War: British Special Forces in North Africa, 1940-1943* (Westport: Praeger, 1987), p. 104.

the only way to get there was by using the main road. This route entailed many risks but the SAS team agreed that they should go for it.

T2 then formed a "fascist convoy" and proceeded to Mersa Brega on the highway, exchanging fascist salutes and greetings with some fifty on-coming trucks before arriving at a crossroads near the anchorage. There they encountered twenty vehicles parked alongside the road, with about sixty men standing around them. Shooting at them with every gun they had for perhaps a quarter of an hour and at very close range, the raiders killed at least 15 of the enemy and wounded many others, without casualty to themselves. While the shooting was still going on, the "parashots" placed time bombs in all the enemy vehicles.

The patrol then continued another 15 kilometres along the road. To prevent pursuit the men on the last truck laid mines in the potholes, which – they could hear – caused seven explosions and probably accounted for that number of enemy vehicles.

Before turning off to the south, T2 cut telephone wires and blew down many poles to disorganize traffic. Enemy aircraft searched for the patrol all next day and twice passed overhead without seeing them. Camouflage skills can save lives!

There was at this point also a general feeling of relief on the Allied side, as the British had managed to destroy enough of Rommel's rapidly shrinking fleet of tanks. On 11 December 1941 Rommel realized that it was best to blow retreat. Tobruk's siege was lifted and Rommel was driven back towards El Agheila, where he had started his African adventure.

Still, T2 patrol had little rest. On Boxing Day they were off from Jalo again, to take two SAS teams to the airfields by "Marble Arch" and Nofilia. On 27 December Lieutenant Bill Fraser and four men were dropped 8 kilometres from "Marble Arch" and the next day Lieutenant Jock Lewes and six men near Nofilia. T2 Patrol commander Morris reported about what happened:

29.12.41. This day we remained in hiding.

30.12.41. About 18.00 hours we picked up Lt. Lewes and his party at the spot where we had left them on the 28th. He mentioned the fact that he had seen three trucks on our tracks earlier in the day, one of them being covered.

31. 12.41. This morning we proceeded back to Marble Arch to pick up Lt. Fraser's party. During the past three days many enemy planes were sighted flying up and down the coast road. About 10.00 hours in open country we were sighted by a Messerschmitt who immediately attacked us with M.G. fire from a height of about 60 feet. We dispersed as quickly as possible. After using up all his ammunition the plane returned to the nearby aerodrome, but shortly afterwards two Stukas and a recce plane came over, bombing and machine-gunning from a low altitude. Incendiary bullets were used and also cannons. By this time we had hidden our cars and camouflaged them as well as possible, but the planes flew low and followed our tracks. My own truck was the first to go, catching fire. Hand grenades, belts of ammunition and petrol then blew up, completely wrecking the vehicle. Another truck was destroyed by a bomb shortly afterwards. From where I was at this time I could see two large columns of smoke from my own and the bombed truck and after a second bomb had been dropped a third lot of smoke was seen in the direction a truck had taken when disappearing. Although I did not actually see the third truck destroyed some of the men on that side of the area reported that this happened. The vehicle unaccounted for,

During sandstorms goggles were a must. Note the sand channels attached to the rear body sides. Photo from June 1942. (Estate of Anthony (Tich) Cave via LRDG Preservation Society)

on which were Gpl. Garven,.Tpr. Brown and Gnr. Stutterd, may have escaped to the south-west and if so should return.

Later two Stukas searched the area, in which there was little cover of any description, using machine-guns and 20mm. cannon over a wide area. At dusk the remaining truck, Tio, was heard to move and we found it. We searched the area for eight miles, calling loudly and flashing lights but could find no one. Lt. Lewes was killed by machine-gun fire in the second attack. Finally we made away to the south as ground patrols could again be heard in the vicinity and there was no cover for many miles in this direction. We, the remainder, which included the four parachutists, travelled in the one surviving truck all this night, crossing the Marada road at 05.00 hours next morning.

1.1.42. Reached Jalo at 17.00 hours.[5]

The killed Lieutenant Lewes had been one of the very first to join SAS and had invented the special bomb for the airfield raiders. They had lacked a combined incendiary and explosive device. Jock Lewes came up with was a small bag with plastic explosive mixed with thermite and a small amount of diesel oil and steel filings. A Lewes bomb, as it became known, would be placed inside the cockpit or on the wing of an aircraft.[6]

5   Kennedy Shaw, p. 128.
6   Ladd, pp. 2-7.

Grease gun treatment

There were surprisingly few deaths among the patrolmen. Tragic as those were, the greater horror was that a patrol would suffer severe medical problems on a long range mission. Let us first recall that patrols were small, usually two officers and about 28 other ranks. After some months of operating it was found that half patrols also could accomplish big things. With such small numbers, and separated from civilization sometimes not by days of travel, but by weeks, every single man counted. One man´s illness would affect the whole mission. Fortunately, really bad medical situations did not happen very often. But when they did, the sick or wounded man´s special knowledge and skills were of course no longer available, plus that his comrades had to help him with his needs. Navigators were, basically, not allowed to get ill.

The medical officer, the doctor, was usually at Group HQ, so while a patrol or half patrol was hundreds of kilometres from proper medical treatment, the "hospital" was the one medical orderly within each patrol. Some of the orderlies had proper training but regardless they all had to improvise. For example, they realized that a grease gun could be used for an enema.

The doctor could in some cases help the men out in the desert via instructions over the radio. On one occasion there were symptoms of appendicitis but thanks to the doctor´s "radio-therapy" the symptoms disappeared.

10

Rommel´s push into Egypt

Operation Crusader had, in the end, done the job and provided the Allies with the first larger victory over German ground forces. Thus Rommel was back where he had started in Tripolitania. Those of his first batch of tanks that had not been destroyed were by this time, after almost a year, severely worn by the desert sand.

The British generals, at this stage, of course, wanted to continue driving the Germans and Italians out of North Africa. That is, after they had done some proper planning. Rommel, however, was not the type of enemy to allow the Allied planning and preparations to be completed.

Rommel fully understood that speed plus willpower could outweigh many other factors. With some newly arrived tanks he started a German offensive on 21 January 1942, pushing surprised Allied units in front of him towards Gazala. There, the frontline stabilized and both sides built up their strength for the giant duel that began on 26 May.[1] While Rommel then let the Italian infantry divisions attack and distract the British near the coast, he brought his armour down to Bir Hacheim where Free French forces under General Koenig resisted Rommel's attacks for a fortnight. At that point the French were ordered to evacuate. The German advance succeeded, but the defence of the French at Bir Hakeim meant a long and vulnerable Axis supply route around the Gazala line. Rommel retired to a defensive position backing onto British minefields, forming a base in the midst of British defences. Italian engineers managed to lift mines from the minefields to create a supply route. The Eighth Army then counter-attacked, failed and the Axis units were able to regain the initiative. The British withdrew from the Gazala Line and the Germans overran Tobruk.

Tobruk fell on 21 June 1942 and this was the direct motive for Rommel´s promotion to field marshal. Rommel exploited the success by pursuing the British into Egypt, towards El Alamein.

But it was also in those dark days that the long awaited, brand new Chevrolet 30-cwt 1533X2 trucks arrived in Cairo for service in the LRDG. They had been specially ordered in Canada according to Bagnold's wishes and would replace the 30-cwt Ford, which consumed too much fuel and copious amounts of oil.

The LRDG arsenal was also improved. Every patrol was equipped with at least six Vickers machine guns, five Lewis machine guns and a captured Italian Breda 20mm anti-aircraft gun.

In this phase approximately half of all the Axis supplies were transported on the only road between Tripoli and Benghazi, the costal road. LRDG's surveillance work there, near "Marble Arch", was therefore a primary source of information about the enemy's movements and strength.[2]

LRDG's more offensive operations were in two areas: one in Cyrenaica's coastal belt along the eastern shore of the Sirte Bay. The second in Tripolitania and Fezzan, west of a line through Sirte. The main targets were fuel dumps and motor vehicles.

---

1   *Special Forces in the Desert War 1940-43*, p. 148.
2   Kennedy Shaw, p. 146.

Two patrols were earmarked to take SAS to enemy airfields. These airfields happened to be around three places starting with the letter B: Berca, Benina and Barce. Simultaneously, cooperation between the LRDG and the Free French increased, especially with French paratroopers.

As the only Allied unit in Siwa Oasis, LRDG became increasingly a servant of other units. This forced Guy Prendergast to write to his superiors in Cairo that:

> [LRDG has] found itself more and more in the position of 'universal aunts' to anyone who has business in the desert behind the enemy lines. An increasing stream of commandos (European and Arab), L Detachment, ISLD, G(R), bogus Germans (Buck), lost travellers, 'escape scheme' promoters, stranded aviators, etc., has continued to arrive at Siwa needing petrol, rations, maintenance, information, training, accommodation, and supplies of all kinds. Their requirements can usually be effected, but not without straining our own resources and staff.[3]

3   Kelly, p. 188.

11

Bye bye Siwa

When Rommel crossed the Egyptian border on 23 June and approached El Alamein it was considered necessary for the LRDG to retreat from Siwa Oasis. Having to leave Siwa was unfortunate, for it had good water, good living quarters and even some ancient pools to bathe in after a hot day in the desert. Siwa was evacuated in the second half of June 1942 and the entire LRDG was regrouped. Group HQ and five patrols would be based in the Nile delta, far from any area of operations. Raiding would be done mainly from Kufra Oasis, behind enemy lines.[1]

A new British raiding campaign was ordered, under SAS commander David Stirling and to be supported by the LRDG. The SAS were now receiving raiding vehicles of their own, US made Jeeps, but they were still relying on the LRDG for the great mass of supplies, as well as navigation and signals.[2]

The first objective for the now largely Jeep-borne SAS with LRDG support was to attack six airfields on the night of 7-8 July. Some targets turned out to be used only during the day or had very few aircraft, while the Bagush airfield was a jackpot. More than 20 German and Italian aircraft were destroyed. But equally important was that the SAS were perfecting the method of destroying parked aircraft. By using Jeeps with several machine guns and driving in some kind of formation it seemed possible to execute raids with greater surprise, speed, indirect protection (by means of a wall of bullets) and effectiveness, than by random shooting and bomb-laying.

The Jeeps were armed with twin Vickers K machine guns, some with Browning machine guns and some with both types. Some had a total of two machine guns, most had three and some had four.

David Stirling and Paddy Mayne took airfield raiding to its logical end by increasing both the number of raiding Jeeps and machine guns, and adding some choreography. To further increase the effectiveness of their planned mass Jeep raid they conducted a live-fire formation driving rehearsal, emphasizing the ability to change positions and directions.

Stirling then headhunted LRDG navigator Mike Sadler and gave him the task of leading 18 SAS Jeeps about 80 kilometres from their hideout, to a Luftwaffe airfield that so far had been spared, Sidi Haneish – not that far from the coast and about 375 kilometres west-northwest of Cairo.

Mike Sadler, originally a Londoner, had not been a navigator before the war, but had listened carefully to Lofty Carr´s crash course in navigating by the stars.

Getting to Sidi Haneish there were Jeep accidents and moments of doubt about the navigation. But sure enough, Mike Sadler took the SAS and his escorting LRDG comrades to the target, reaching it the night of 26-27 July.

Just before the Sidi Haneish attack, David Stirling´s final instructions were:

---

1   Lloyd Owen, p. 96.
2   *Special Forces in the Desert War 1940-43*, p. 161.

At the edge of the aerodrome form a line abreast and all guns spray the area – when I advance follow me in your two columns and on my green Very light open fire outwards at the aircraft. Follow exactly in each other´s tracks 5 yards apart, speed not more than 4 mph – return to the rendezvous independently moving only at night.[3]

With 60 guns firing at them simultaneously during about 15 minutes there was simply not much opportunity for the guarding German troops to shoot back. They did of course get some bullets in the air too, but nothing close to the storm of lead unleashed by the Jeeps driving in formation. There was one SAS casualty. It was believed that the Germans lost 30 aircraft and that some more were damaged.

The escorting LRDG trucks were followed by German vehicles as well as a German Storch reconnaissance aircraft. The Storch descended, assuming the trucks were German, only to be captured by the patrol. In spite of several misgivings, all trucks made it back.

Mike Sadler, the LRDG navigator that had guided the mass Jeep raid, was retained by David Stirling and thus went from LRDG to SAS service, where he soon was made an officer.

The belief that the Sidi Haneish raid resulted in the loss of 30 German aircraft plus more damaged was a bit optimistic, the official tally was determined to be 18 aircraft destroyed and a further 12 damaged. Still, this number too certainly affected Luftwaffe operations in the area (few of the damaged aircraft can have seen service soon) and the raid was a milestone for all those involved. But at the first real debrief David Stirling chose to stress that the job could have gone even better, saying: "It wasn´t nearly good enough! Some of you were out of position, some of you were firing at planes you could only just see, and a lot of you were firing wildly."[4]

Many years later David Stirling told his biographer Alan Hoe: "Privately I was very pleased, but I didn´t want the men to become to blasé about the business."[5]

The Germans believed that Sidi Haneish airfield was attacked by armoured reconnaissance vehicles – this has emerged from a Luftwaffe war diary. Obviously, the chaos created by the constant stream of bullets kept the Germans from properly identifying the vehicles and so they assumed they had been attacked by armoured cars. The Jeeps were certainly heavily armed, but did not have even the smallest armour plate.

Mike Sadler, the LRDG navigator behind the triumph at Sidi Haneish, is at the time of writing (2018) the last living veteran of the raid. In a 2017 interview to the BBC Sadler said of David Stirling: "He was not concentrating so much on the job in hand. He was thinking much more on higher matters."

Indian Long Range Squadron

Although the British in North Africa had to retreat several times during the first half of 1942, Ralph Bagnold somehow still found time to help create an Indian copy of the LRDG, the Indian Long Range Squadron (ILRS).[6] Of course, this was not done without reason. There was a real fear among the Allied top commanders that the Germans would defeat the Soviet troops in the Caucasus and continue from there into Persia and Iraq. The ILRS was therefore formed to patrol in the latter countries.

---

3   Mortimer (2015:2), p. 48.
4   Mortimer (2015:2), pp. 68-69.
5   Hoe, p. 178.
6   *Special Forces in the Desert War 1940-43*, p. 183.

Like the LRDG, the ILRS consisted of volunteers. The unit started training in early 1942 and joined an LRDG patrol from Siwa to Trigh el Abd to get to know real working conditions. It then patrolled behind enemy lines from Siwa, Kufra and Hon. The ILRS finally consisted of four patrols.[7]

7   Moreman, pp. 60-61.

12

Operation Agreement

In September 1942 Operation Agreement was launched, mainly against Rommels's forces in Tobruk. The operation included a series of supporting ground and amphibious operations, carried out by British, Rhodesian and New Zealand forces, not least the LRDG.[1]

The main objective was to destroy harbour facilities, ships, airfields, large oil depots and to capture Jalo Oasis.

John Haselden, the Arabic-speaking and Arab-looking SOE agent, this time had a rather large force under him, travelling in four trucks of their own, sporting German markings. But to get to their targets, inside Tobruk, they needed guidance from Y1 Patrol under Captain David Lloyd Owen. On the night of 13/14 September they set out and attracted little attention as they passed Axis traffic. Five kilometres from Tobruk they parted with their LRDG guides.

Y1 Patrol was on its way to the position they were supposed to wait for Haselden in, when suddenly a German staff car appeared and the patrolmen promptly shot it to pieces. One of the passengers survived for a while and told his captors that Tobruk was expecting a raid. But Y1 had no radio contact with Haselden´s force and thus could only wait for them as instructed.

The night was filled with sounds that Y1 had hoped not to hear, the sound of the guns in Tobruk that Haselden´s raiders should have silenced. Y1 waited and waited but finally had to return to Kufra, where they eventually could piece together what had happened to Haselden and his men. They had been able to pass a large number of enemy troops and had attacked their first objective which was a small villa, killing or driving off the Italians holding it. They then knocked out several machine gun positions and a radio station. In the early morning of 14 September they signaled for "Force C" to land, but only two of the 16 motor torpedo boats were able to land reinforcements as the enemy fire was, by now, very heavy. Despite the lack of reinforcement the group managed to knock out four anti- aircraft guns by rolling grenades down the barrels.[2]

With no support forthcoming and with ammunition running low, Haselden ordered his men to attempt to break out with every man for himself. He led a charge with five men following him against encroaching Italian forces, but was killed by a hand grenade. Only six of Haselden´s men made it back to British lines.

The deaths were the result of too many people knowing too much about the "top secret" raid – which was a much larger disaster than first became apparent to the patrolmen. During the operation the British side lost several hundred killed and captured, four motor torpedo boats, two destroyers and several small amphibious craft.

---

1   *Special Forces in the Desert War 1940-43*, p. 167.
2   Lloyd Owen, p 104.

LRDG jeep and a Chevrolet moving to Barce. Aside from Vickers Ks the patrolmen have a small grenade launcher attached to a rifle. (LRDG Preservation Society)

Rest for Y patrol after the Hon raid in Tripolitania, September 1942. (Estate of Anthony (Tich) Cave via LRDG Preservation Society)

Help from "Popski"

To support Operation Agreement, the smaller Operation Caravan was launched with LRDG at the tip of the spear. This raiding force under the command of Major Jake Easonsmith mainly consisted of the patrols G1 and T1, a total of 47 patrolmen in 12 Chevrolet 30-cwt trucks and five Jeeps to attack the Italian airfield just northeast of the town of Barce.[3] To somewhat ease the challenge of attacking the airfield, a diversionary attack was planned against the main Campo Maddelena barracks south-west of Barce, and the railway station to the south of the town.

The LRDG patrols were supported by a Jeep-borne Arab-looking officer, Vladimir Peniakoff, better known as just "Popski". He had been born in Belgium to Russian parents, had been a volunteer soldier for France during WWI and during the interwar period he had established himself in Egypt as an engineer with a sugar manufacturer.[4] In Egypt he had learnt to navigate in the desert and picked up a few more languages, so that he spoke English, Russian, Italian, German, French and Arabic. "Popski" and two Senussi Bedouins had collected fresh and useful local information in the area just before the raid.[5]

The raiding force reached the outskirts of Barce on 13 September and established a well-camouflaged camp among some trees. Captain Nick Wilder and his Kiwi T1 Patrol got the biggest task, to raid the airfield which air photographs had shown to be in full use. Skirting round the outskirts of the town he came to the air base. At the entrance Wilder stopped, jumped off his truck, opened the gate and drove in. Some Italian troops came running and were immediately shot down. Then a large petrol tanker caught fire and lit up the area rather nicely. Wilder came to what must have been the mess buildings and threw some hand grenades into the windows. Now he could focus on the aircraft.

In single file he led the patrol from his Jeep around the airfield firing incendiary at each airplane. The last truck had the job, with short-delay-action bombs, to blow up aircraft which had not already caught fire.

The Italian troops fired away at the intruders but without causing any harm. After a while a mortar joined in, but that did not help them. After about an hour of this Wilder had visited in turn 32 aircraft, of which twenty were definitely alight and the rest damaged. When his ammunition was running short he left, without any of his men having been hit.

The problems started on the way home, when the patrols were repeatedly subjected to well-aimed aviation attacks that destroyed 10 of the 12 Chevrolets and left many patrolmen injured. There followed a repeat of "Moore's March", but the two patrolmen who walked the farthest, 240 kilometers, were unfortunately captured the Italians.

Based on Captain Nick Wilder's report it was thought that T1 patrol had destroyed or damaged 32 aircraft, mainly bombers. An Italian report stated 16 aircraft destroyed and seven damaged and this was later accepted as the result. These figures said nothing about the severe damage done to many military vehicles, buildings and an unknown number of casualties. However, the Barce raid, as it has become known, did result in the awarding of two Distinguished Service Orders, one Military Cross, and three Military Medals. The recipients of the Distinguished Service Orders for the Barce raid were the overall commander of the operation, Captain Jake Easonsmith, and, of course, Captain Nick Wilder. Only two more times did LRDG officers receive the DSO.[6]

---

3   Lloyd Owen, p. 105.
4   Vladimir Peniakoff, *Popski's Private Army* (London: The Reprint Society, 1953), p. 3.
5   Lloyd Owen, p. 105.
6   Kennedy Shaw, p. 242.

The spy services of "Popski" (the name LRDG signallers gave Vladimir Peniakoff) obviously were appreciated by the LRDG and SAS, because shortly after his support to them at Barce he was allowed to form No. 1 Demolition Squadron, which became better known as Popski's Private Army and was a smaller version of the LRDG/SAS. It was created to specifically attack Rommel's petrol dumps during General Montgomery's offensive at El Alamein.

The First Battle of El Alamein, which lies just 240 kilometres northwest of Cairo, had taken place during July 1942. Rommel's most important supply base was still Tripoli, more than 2,000 kilometres away, which meant that after the Allies had halted the Axis advance a stalemate ensued. In August, Winston Churchill visited Cairo on his way to meet Josef Stalin in Moscow. He decided to replace General Claude Auchinleck with General William Gott. But the latter was killed when his aircraft was shot down. He was hastily replaced with General Bernard Montgomery. Thus, in the Second Battle of El Alamein, that started on 23 October 1942, Rommel confronted "Monty".

Hitler sent an order to Rommel on 3 November that ended with the words: "As to your troops, you can show them no other road than that to victory or death." More or less knowing what the telegram would say, Rommel postponed reading it. His retreat was probably inevitable given his extremely long supply chain and faced with Allied numerical superiority plus superior Allied handling of air support to ground forces.

On 11 November Rommel was out of Egypt and the German retreat continued into Libya. The Second Battle of El Alamein revived the morale of Allied forces all over the world, and coincided with the Allied invasion of French North Africa, which started on 8 November.

13

The fall of Fezzan

During the last five months of the LRDG´s desert war, the focus was constantly moving westwards. This was both because of the German retreat through Libya and the success of the Allied invasion of French Morocco and Algeria. After just a few days the troops of the French Vichy regime in Morocco had joined the Allies.

When General Philippe Leclerc's 2nd Armoured Division took part in the liberation of Paris in August 1944, world history was written. Not quite as well known is how the LRDG from November 1942 guided the French general on his march from Chad deep into Libya.[1] This strike from the south against Tripoli was something that the Free French had been wanting to do for a very long time, but the appearance and incredible advances of the German expeditionary force for Africa had made it hard for the British to allocate supporting forces to a rather peripheral region like Fezzan (southwest Libya).

With the Axis in general retreat and crisis the time had come for LRDG to facilitate a Free French attack by means of attaching five patrols to Leclerc´s forces on the border between Chad and Libya.

The French had asked for Allied air cover but none was available at the time. The patrolmen would simply have to be extra vigilant in spotting aircraft and then either find cover or shoot them down.

It was S2 Patrol with six Chevrolets and 18 men under the command of Lieutenant James Henry that first came to the area. Soon after having linked up with the French in Fezzan and observed their lack of desert driving skills, they were headed for Gatrun Oasis in the Murzuk district. In his diary, James Henry wrote about how the action started on 26 December:

> Arrived in sight of Gatrun at daybreak. Two French trucks and S2 advanced towards the oasis to see what would happen. Enemy opened up field artillery and Bredas of various calibres. Rest of column came up and then moved slowly eastwards in artillery formation until we were just out of range. French 75mm sent a few rounds back.
>
> The column then moved eastwards to a range of hills twenty miles away, dispersed and held a council of war. The original plan was to shell Gatrun sufficiently to shake up the garrison and then by-pass it, leaving the main body to capture it.
>
> Just before lunch S2 patrol with a French patrol was sent out with the idea of doing a recce of the northern part of the oasis, just out of artillery range, and to lure out any [Italian] *Auto Saharan* company and lead them into range of the French 75's in position near the hills.
>
> We got to within a couple of miles of the oasis when we were attacked by six fighters and two bombers with machine gun fire and bombs. The desert was good going so we fought back, gradually edging off towards the hills and dodging bombs during our spare moments.

---

1   *Special Forces in the Desert War 1940-43*, p. 185.

Saw a column of black smoke rising several miles north of us. My gunner said it was an aircraft burning though he had not actually seen the crash.

Soon afterwards ground strafing ceased but bombing continued for some time. During the fight we picked up one Frenchman and four *askaris* [native troops] whose truck had been put out of action.

Checked up on the movements of the S2 trucks, one unaccounted for, so circled back to look for it and found it heading back to look for me. [We] had reached talking distance when the bomber started work on us again; kept visual contact and returned to the hills. Carter came across with information that two French trucks had been damaged and one *askari* killed. A Frenchman in the patrol said he had seen the aircraft crash and since ours were the only trucks that fired Col. Ingold credited us with shooting it down and complimented us on the calm and organized way in which we had met the attack, saying that we had set an excellent example to the French troops.[2]

S2 Patrol were again in combat on 28 December by the oasis of Umm el Araneb, against both Italian aircraft and an *Auto Saharan* company. But the Italians were no longer in a fighting mood. Thanks largely to the French artillery they simply departed and the local garrison surrendered on 4 January 1943.

The earlier circumvented oasis town of Gatrun surrendered on January 6 and the Italians in Murzuk gave up two days later. Thus Fezzan fell and there was not much left in the south to disturb the forces heading along the coast towards Tripoli.

2   Kennedy Shaw, p. 230.

14

Wilder's Gap

LRDG's road surveillance work on the coastal road had become increasingly valued in 1942, but as the Germans retreated in larger numbers, the only coast road was filled with units that stopped and lingered close to the observation posts, sometimes almost on top of them. The work was not mainly physically inconvenient, but mentally exhausting. There had always been a risk of falling ill with the infamous desert madness or *cafard* that sometimes overcomes legionnaires stationed in desolate desert outposts. But now the road watchers had to put up with near constant risk of being detected.

In 1942 the daily number of enemy vehicles in both directions was during several months in the hundreds, but with the Axis in full retreat the number could be thousands of vehicles per day, that all had to be observed, noted and identified. Virtually all vehicles were heading west. These figures, and the fact that hardly any troops were going east, confirmed Monty's assumption that Rommel was completely evacuating Cyrenaica. This was further confirmed when civilians with their furniture appeared. The Italian settlers too were being evacuated from Cyrenaica.

At the beginning of December Monty and his Eighth Army was on the border between the two main Libyan regions, Cyrenaica and Tripolitania, standing before El Agheila and ready to push Rommel out of his positions there, that formed a defensive line between some salt marshes and the sea.[1] A frontal attack on such strong positions would be costly. Montgomery therefore chose a manoeuvre often used by both sides in the desert war, the turning of the southern flank. In this case it meant an advance across country that LRDG had first explored on the way to the Sirte desert in 1941, and which the patrols had afterwards got to know well on their way to and from the classic road watch. So, who could better guide the 2nd New Zealand Division and the 4th Light Armoured Brigade through this area than the LRDG? Naturally, the patrol chosen was from New Zealand, Captain Tony Browne's R1 Patrol.

Montgomery's initial plan was that his outflanking "left hook" move would start on 15 December, but on learning that enemy reinforcements were on their way Monty had it start on 13 December, Browne's patrol began leading their assigned division of countrymen plus a brigade in a 400 kilometre arc around the German positions at El Agheila. Having done this, R1 Patrol on 17 December guided the New Zealand Division in another flanking manoeuvre, around Nofilia. The enemy was then, to quote Monty, "severely mauled by the New Zealanders".

New Zealand General Freyberg later wrote that "success of the operation depended upon negotiating a hitherto [by large military units] uncrossed desert".

Tripoli fell on 23 January 1943, exactly three months since the start of the Second Battle of El Alamein. But already a week before Tripoli's fall the LRDG had been inside Tunisia. The first patrol being the Kiwi T1 Patrol led by Captain Nick Wilder.[2] They had been told to try to find a route through the hills running south from Matmata, so that large military formations could be moved on to the plain to the west. (Much later, Matmata was featured in two episodes of "Star Wars").

---

1   *Special Forces in the Desert War 1940-43*, p. 190.
2   *Special Forces in the Desert War 1940-43*, p. 194.

Searching for this key route, Captain Wilder ran into some very bad "going", but decided to leave his Jeep and continue searching on foot. After a lengthy walk he made a discovery.

Montgomery's main wish at this point was to outflank the French-built "Mareth Line", also called a smaller version of the more famous French Maginot Line.[3] It consisted of several strong-points with all-round defence, and had been designed to hold out for a considerable period of time.   Naturally, LRDG and SAS patrols as well as RAF photo-reconnaissance aircraft were all sent out to find a way through the Matmata Hills. And not just any way but a route capable of withstanding the passage of many thousand marching soldiers and some 6000 wheeled and tracked vehicles and heavy guns.

The passage that was eventually found not by the RAF or SAS but by LRDG Captain Nick Wilder became known as "Wilder's Gap" and is located about 50 kilometres to the south-west of Tataouine, the town that later became Tatooine in the "Star Wars" films.

Much to the dismay of T1 Patrol, they were denied the honour of leading the New Zealand Corps through the gap, as Captain Wilder had been recalled for duty with the Kiwi Cavalry. However, Captain Ron Tinker and three other men from T2 patrol in two Jeeps remained to act as LRDG guides for the outflanking operation.

Montgomery issued the following message to the men of the 8th Army on 15 March 1943, the eve of the offensive against the Mareth Line:

In the battle that is now to start, the Eighth Army will destroy the enemy now facing us in the Mareth positions; will burst through the Gabès gap; will then drive northwards on to Sfax, Sousse, and finally to Tunis. We will not stop or let up until Tunis has been captured and the enemy has either give up the struggle or has been pushed into the sea.[4]

The New Zealand Corps began the outflanking on 19 March, guided by Captain Tinker and his men. The Corps passed through Wilder's Gap and paused in an assembly area while the further route was plotted. One wadi seemed just too steep, but Tinker and Captain Goodsir of the New Zealand Engineers found a place where tracks could be made by machinery to get vehicles across. The NZ Corps left the assembly area the day before Eighth Army launched its frontal attack on the Mareth Line. It then advanced to Tebaga along a route chosen by the LRDG, and clashed with the enemy on the 21 March.

The patrolmen remained with the NZ Corps until Gabes was reached after fierce fighting. With some help from the RAF and their American colleagues, Gabes fell on 29 March. The following morning, in the British House of Commons, Winston Churchill said: "General Montgomery's decision to throw his weight on to the turning movement instead of persisting in a frontal attack has been crowned with success."

On the same day, General Montgomery sent the following message to General Freyberg:

My very best congratulations to NZ Corps and 10th Corps on splendid results achieved by the left hook. These results have led to the complete disintegration of the enemy resistance and the whole Mareth position. Give my congratulations to all your officers and men, and tell them how pleased I am with all they have done.

---

3   Ken Ford, *The Mareth Line 1943* (Oxford: Osprey, 2012), p. 44.
4   Herbert Charles O'Neill, *The tide turns* (London: Faber and Faber, 1944), p. 174.

In a letter to the Commanding Officer, LRDG, i.e. Colonel Prendergast, dated 2 April 1943, General Montgomery wrote:

> I would like you to know how much I appreciate the excellent work done by your patrols and by the SAS in reconnoitering the country up to the Gabes gap. Without your careful and reliable reports the launching of the "left hook" by the NZ [Corps] would have been a leap in the dark; with the information they produced, the operation could be planned with some certainty, and as you know, went off without a hitch . . . please give my thanks to all concerned and best wishes from EIGHTH ARMY for the new tasks you are undertaking.[5]

LRDG recalled to Egypt

The enemy had not yet capitulated in North Africa, the last Axis units in Tunisia capitulated only on 13 May 1943. But the terrain beyond Gabes was deemed unsuitable for LRDG work and the unit was therefore recalled to Egypt, where most LRDG patrolmen arrived in early April .

For two and a half years LRDG had been the masters of the inner desert, moving through it as they pleased, causing the enemy losses out of all proportion to their own. But there was no desert fighting left to do, it seemed. The war was far from over and smart soldiers were needed on other fronts. Of course, it was remembered that these men had been borrowed from other units, not least NZ units. These units were keen to get back their men as soon as possible. However, it was decided to not disband LRDG and many patrolmen thus went on to serve in the LRDG/SAS in Greece, Yugoslavia and Italy. Their work was largely in the intelligence gathering domain and they often cooperated with local partisans. But that is another story.

The driver of this LRDG vehicle is unknown (and his scorpion badge is not visible) but the passenger is Paddy MacKay of T1 patrol, who is wearing LRDG slip-on shoulder titles on his battle dress blouse. Note the sun compass in front of him. (LRDG Preservation Society)

5   Kennedy Shaw, p. 238; *Special Forces in the Desert War 1940-43*, p. 212.

Part Two

Reenacting in Egypt and the LRDG Legacy

15

In the Tracks of the Ghost Patrol

During eighteen days in April 2012, a small group of enthusiasts realized a common dream, they wished to experience something similar to the classic desert voyages of the Long Range Desert Group. We were going to drive in the tracks of the Ghost Patrol, in two completely authentic Jeeps. Virtually every part of the chosen vehicles had been made during the Second World War.

I myself, Karl-Gunnar Norén, faced one of my life's biggest challenges. Honestly speaking, I was pretty nervous. How would it go? Would we really be able to cross the Great Sand Sea up to Siwa, a distance as long as between Stockholm and Gothenburg? Would my driving abilities stand up to the big test in the sand, in one of the world's largest deserts?

The challenge also had a social side. Of the other expedition members I had only met Toby and John, during one single training weekend in England a few months earlier. Generally speaking, for all participants, we had only had limited contact with each other.

We were three Brits, three Americans and one Swede – I, the sole author of this chapter – plus the Egyptian tour leader who had a logistics group of three people needed to make the expedition a pretty safe one. A small but rather heavily armed patrol from the Egyptian Army would join us after the Dakhla Oasis and on our behalf respond to undefined threats.

So, during two weeks, seven middle aged men in two Jeeps built in 1943 would try to relive the atmosphere of the legendary Long Range Desert Group. But with zero risk of encountering Luftwaffe aircraft.

The general idea was to drive along and sometimes over the giant sand dunes in the Great Sand Sea. We also wanted to visit some special places by the south and southwestern side of Gilf el Kebir, a mountain plateau the size of a small country.

We looked forward to camp under the stars hundreds of kilometres from all cities and to stand in the "Cave of Swimmers" made famous by the movie "The English Patient" and gaze at the nine-thousand-year-old cave paintings. Last but not least we wished to discover remains of the foremost desert unit ever – and especially of their vehicles.

We wanted to end the adventure in the Spitfire Bar, the same bar as in "An ice cold in Alexandria", a classic film about survival during the desert war, filmed not long after the war.

It would not be a comfortable trip along the Mediterranean coast. We were not interested in visiting any bathing resort in Sharm el Sheikh. We wanted to be in the real desert, to experience lots of sweat, and get that special feeling one gets after a hard day of driving in the desert. However, with support by a local logistics team that would provide us with food and guidance through some of the most splendid landscapes on the planet.

We assumed that our mandatory military escort was a small contribution to the funding of the Egyptian Armed Forces. None of us knew that 23 Egyptian border guards had disappeared without trace in the areas we would visit, just before the expedition's departure.

The idea of an expedition in connection with the 70th anniversary of Long Range Desert Group operations first came to the three British team members. In order to realize the project, they invited four "paying guests", both for financial reasons and to add specialist knowledge and experience.

The British trio consisted primarily of Toby Savage, a professional photographer with many years of experience with archaeologists in Libya and Egypt. Add to that a great sense of humor and great enthusiasm for Land Rovers and Jeeps. Toby owned both the Jeeps from 1943 we were to travel in. One was a Willys, the other a Ford. Together with his son Matt Savage, who owns a firm specialized in 4x4, Toby had restored them to an amazing level.

Toby's closest co-worker was the skilled engineer John Carrol, with great love for both two-wheel and four-wheel drive vehicles. John is a freelance journalist with 4x4 vehicles as a specialty. He works with both pen and camera. Great photographer. What he does not know about cars is not worth knowing.

The third British gentleman was Sam Watson, a teacher at the international school in Cairo and with extensive desert experience. Since the supply of deserts in the UK is very limited, Sam lives in Cairo and, just like LRDG founder Ralph Bagnold, spends much of his spare time in the desert. However, not in a T-Ford but a little more modern and rather specially equipped Land Rover Series III. Can handle Cairo traffic!

One of the three Yankees in the expedition was Rick Péwé, without exaggeration one of the world's most experienced 4x4 specialists. Not because he owns 19 Jeeps, or because he is the editor of a 4x4 magazine, but because he can repair just everything in an engine. In my whole life, I have never seen such commitment, such skills and enthusiasm for engine problems!

Then there was Bob Atwater, an experienced member of the truly exclusive American association Explorers Club. As a former member of the US Marine Corps he is a strong character. Bob was equipped with extensive experience of deserts, terrain vehicles and expeditions. He needs a number of eggs for breakfast.

Expedition participant Jason Paterniti is also a member of the Explorers Club and brought great knowledge of deserts and desert driving, as well as a scientific and methodical approach. Jason performed the expedition's many calculations – ranging from travel distances and positions to the carefully calculated fuel consumption of the Jeeps.

I myself contributed experience of deserts in Egypt, Libya and Namibia, but at the start of our adventure had only insignificant experience of driving a car in the desert. Instead, my studies of the archives of Ralph Bagnold came in handy.

The local expedition leader, Mahmud Marai, a professional tour operator with many expeditions behind him, was responsible for food, water, fuel, living quarters in the desert and hotels in Bahariya, Dakla and Siwa Oasis, as well as in Alexandria and Giza. His team consisted of: Tarek abd el Fatah, car driver, mechanic and cook; Mohammed Sabry, food logistics; and truck driver Islam Samir. How did they do? Several weeks of meals and no sand at all in the food is pretty remarkable, fantastic work!

Our two Jeeps, Willys MB 1943 and Ford GPW 1943, were almost identical, one must be an expert to see the difference. LRDG used exactly the same Jeeps as of 1942. During the Second World War, there were few light vehicles that could compete with the Jeep in off-road characteristics and reliability. They were not going to disappoint us.

Our travel agency's both Toyota Land Cruisers were of a simpler model with a robust interior. Fewer things that can cause trouble, but the same wonderful off-road characteristics. Good for any situation. We took turns riding in one of the Land Cruisers because the Jeeps under these conditions were for three people. Finally, the expedition had a brand new 4x4 Iveco truck for fuel, water, camping equipment and cooking items.

The Egyptian Army Patrol, in its own Land Cruiser, was led by a police major with the appropriate name Sherif Hassan. His subordinates were more anonymous. Their style was basically civilian, they did not wear their uniforms and their assault rifles, Kalashnikovs, were constantly in their car together with a heavier weapon, a machine gun in a sports bag.

The interaction between the cars and the people in the desert became an experience in itself. The expedition was in motion during most of the daytime, often at a speed of 50-60 kilometres per hour. The order of the six vehicles varied all the time and depended on the terrain. At times the column would be stretched out, only to quickly drive in a rather tight formation. The basic rule was to be within "eye-shot". We were always looking backwards, counting the vehicles and making sure nobody was left behind with engine problems. We had no internal radio communication, so we had to use our eyes – just like the LRDG.

Without reliable cars and skilled travel mechanics, no desert trips. It is hardly realistic today to mobilize the seventy camels that would be required, or spend the six months that would take the same expedition without motor vehicles. Even though the Jeeps demanded some work, none of the "aging ladies" broke down. Strong proof of how clever the Jeep's basic design is.

Here follow excerpts from my and some other participants' diaries and notes:

Thursday, 5 April

When I landed at Cairo International in the afternoon Toby Savage and some of the other expedition members had already been in Egypt for a few days, to get the Jeeps out from the port of Alexandria. I was able to get myself to Mena House Hotel in Ghiza, within sight of the Pyramid of Cheops. At this legendary hotel Churchill had slept, and this was where the peace talks between Israel and Egypt began in 1977.

In the evening, all the expedition participants had arrived at the hotel and we immediately started chatting. A nice, promising bunch.

Tomorrow the Jeeps will be driven from Alexandria to Mena House and our expedition will start the 16-day and 1,600-kilometer-long journey through the desert on Friday. We bring with us everything we might need. Our plan is that after the Dakhla Oasis we enter the desert and drive west to the southern part of the mountain range Gilf Kebir and explore the traces of Long Range Desert Group missions and visit caves with 9,000 year old paintings from the period when the area had a completely different climate, with vegetation and a rich wildlife. But we also have the ambition to investigate some interesting observations from satellite imagery to perhaps discover something so far unknown.

After Gilf Kebir, we will head over the Great Sand Sea to the legendary oasis of Siwa through a landscape that alternately consists of easygoing ground that allows for driving at 50-60 kilometres per hour, and more demanding dunes. From Siwa we plan to drive on common roads to Alexandria and finally Cairo. The two Jeeps will then be transported to the UK in a container. This is the plan, but the trick is to adapt the plan to reality.

Friday, 6 April

The Jeeps that actually were to arrive on 27 March were first unloaded yesterday and the paperwork to get a customs clearance, travel permit and temporary Egyptian car registration is estimated to take three days. Fridays are, as you might know, a Muslim holy day, so despite the arrival of the

Jeeps, we cannot get them out. Instead, we visit Cairo's suburb Mazarra and see the house Pat Clayton lived in when he worked in the city. In the early LRDG days, a lot of plans must have been made in this house. We then got ourselves four Land Rovers and went to Wadi Degla on the outskirts of Cairo, a piece of preserved wilderness similar to the terrain we are going to. Our more oceanographic-oriented expedition participants could see traces of freshwater snails that manage to survive between the rain in this desert landscape. The birds also appreciate them.

The remains of a jerrycan reminded us what we really are looking for: traces of the Long Range Desert Group. We are in the area where the newly arrived New Zealand recruits got their first lessons in desert driving!

Saturday, 7 April

A very early departure from Mena House for those of us who are to pick up the Jeeps in Alexandria. At 11.30 we are outside the port office waiting for Toby to get out the Jeeps. But the container with the Jeeps has been delivered to another destination in Alexandria! Hours pass, and all service ends at three o'clock. We have to go back to Mena House without our goods.

Sunday, 8 April

Toby, Rick, Jason and Mahmud left Mena House to go to Alexandria at six o'clock in the morning but did not get the Jeeps until one o'clock, and after customs treatment, car registration, lunch and refueling left "Alex" only late in the afternoon and then took off on a direct road to the oasis Bahariya 775 kilometers south of Alex. During the journey they repaired a broken cooler coupling with steel wire, an aid that, together with duct tape, solves many a problem. Bob, Sam and myself, i.e. the rest of the expedition, left Mena House later in the evening in the Toyota Land Cruisers and drove to the same oasis. A couple of hours before midnight our two groups were united at a petrol station along the road, driving the last stretch in a column. We arrived at Paradise Hotel at dawn, got our rooms and a few hours of sleep.

Monday, 9 April

We are behind schedule, but in our plan we do have some extra days, so we are not worried. After a quick breakfast, we continued to the Dakhla Oasis another 470 kilometers south. About halfway, we had lunch in the Farafra Oasis and then continued to a petrol station where we bought petrol which later turned out to have water in it. With one Jeep emitting a knocking sound we still managed to reach Dakhla late at night.

Having reached Dakhla we realized that the Egyptian bureaucracy was not completely finished with us, a signature was lacking for the military check point to let us leave the paved road further down the desert at the point where the army patrol awaits us. Their fax machine is broken (since January, it turned out later) and Islam (that is his name) from the Egyptian team will have to spend the night on a 200-kilometer journey to obtain the necessary signature. The rest of are sick tired after both a lot of waiting and driving in Jeeps and Land Cruisers and go to bed. Particularly the night driving is stressful, as encountering cars often have poor lights and suddenly donkey carts appear, with dangling kerosen lamps, on the wrong side of the road too. The traffic accident statistics in Egypt are just horrific, 12,000 deaths annually.

Tuesday, 10 April

After some really good sleep, we had a joint meeting around maps and plans to contemplate our not so great situation: we are three days behind schedule, and have to revise our plans and cancel visiting some of the places at Gilf Kebir. All changes must be decided now, before the journey through the Great Sand Sea begins. Out there nothing can be changed, because we have to get to the Siwa Oasis. We then cannot go back. Worrying also that the Jeeps were taken straight from the container and driven some 1,000 kilometers without us first, as we had originally planned, going through them during a day. With a long sea voyage behind it, unexpected things can happen with a car.

A possible complication is that, although most of us have good desert experience, we come from quite different cultures and have, aside from a few short training sessions in England, not worked together. Perhaps the most important thing is that, in an effort to create good relations and equality, we have not established a clear management structure and delegation of tasks and roles. This is an issue that no doubt can cause problems if it is not resolved. We discuss and arrive at a work and responsibility distribution that feels right.

At five, the cars were in order, the paperwork was ready and we could leave the military checkpoint outside of Dakhla. Then we drove more than 100 kilometers, until we could not drive anymore due to the darkness. Major Sharif is not willing to lift the ban on our expedition to travel in the dark. We leave the road and make our first camp in the desert.

Wednesday, 11 April

After a breakfast made by our excellent cooks, we hit the road again to pass the last military checkpoint before we could definitely leave the road. We released air from the tires, changed from 3 kilos to 1.6 kilos and moved out into the Libyan desert, a part of the vast Sahara. The real adventure can begin!

The Ford Jeep suffered from the water-poisoned petrol, and Rick adjusted the ignition to compensate for this. We decided to still consume the bad petrol in the car and jerrycan, to save the good petrol in the accompanying Iveco. It carries a whole cubic meter, 1 000 litres.

After about 70 kilometers, Mahmud brought us to one of LRDG's old petrol depots, where a number of Second World War flimsies were still stacked. Our first contact with the real Long Range Desert Group in its natural element. Soon we would not lift our eyebrows for flimsies, we would find plenty. Here we also found a jar marked "Nestlé Evaporated milk 7/7/42" and a corned beef can from Argentina, unmistakable evidence that Allied soldiers had been here.

After another 17 kilometers, we reached the first remains of one of the LRDG's patrol vehicles, first documented by desert traveler Carlo Bergmann in 2007, during one of his camel expeditions. It is a 6-cylinder Chevrolet engine marked 838773 Gm J-17-16 with the cylinder block number XR3758456. Around the corner there are four tires, some bottles, tin cans and flimsies. If the remains are from a 30-cwt 1939 Egyptian Chevrolet or a 1942 Canadian Chevrolet we could not decide, but thanks to the engine number, we may find out later.

After another three kilometers going south we reach the hill with the plaque commemorating the men of the LRDG and stating that the former commander of Y Patrol (and from 1943 all patrols), David Lloyd Owen and his team at this place in 1983 recovered "Waikaha", a Chevrolet WB 133-inch 4x2 30-cwt truck that eventually came to rest in the Imperial War Museum in London, where it can still be seen today. It is said to be the only original LRDG vehicle on display in a museum, although some of us desert enthusiasts believe that there is also a genuine LRDG vehicle in the El Alamein Museum.

Mahmud believes that the tracks we now follow are original tracks from the LRDG and not tourist tracks, which seems unlikely but might be confirmed by the fact that we found a rare spade labeled NSW, nearby. That means it's from Australian New South Wales. The fact that the spade was still there and had not been removed says a lot about how untouched this area is since the days of the Second World War.

After another 100 kilometers of driving on good ground we discover a former LRDG camp, which, according to Mahmud, was later used by the Egyptian military. Here we find some interesting stuff, including a rare food ration flimsie, the flimsie that the quartermaster packed patrol rations in. The patrolmen ate sumptuously compared to everyone else in the British Army. They received a richly varied diet and even got some evening rum. Here we also actually found an original Molotov cocktail. A glass bottle filled with gasoline and oil and with a kind of wick. Just like those used by the LRDG against some of the enemy's parked aircraft during raids behind enemy lines.

Darkness comes quickly at these latitudes, after an eventful first day in the desert we camped at the position N34.02.252, E27.35.449.

Although we are still far from the Great Sand Sea, our camp is beside a beautiful sand dune.

Thursday, 12 April

Today's plan was originally to get to the LRDG airfield "Eight Bells", but Major Sherif now informed us that 23 Egyptian border guards had disappeared without trace in this area, earlier this month. Our military friends assume that Tubu rebels linked to the Berber clan Guraan are the culprits. Today's Tubu are quite often smugglers of both goods and people - people who travel to Libya to try to get to Europe. The Tubu wish to be left alone with their business and Westerners should be alert. Sherif talked over the satellite phone with Cairo superiors who obviously do not want us to move south of the 23th degree, even though we actually have permission to do so. We continue.

After only 16 kilometers of driving, the first car stopped without apparent reason, and our imagination began to run wild. We imagined rebels attacking in swarms down the dunes to kidnap us and claim millions of dollars from our loved ones. Then one of the Land Cruisers began to slowly move forward again. Mahmud in the second Land Cruiser returned to us and when he got out his face was very serious. We feared the worst, but he told us that a so far unknown LRDG wreck was a little further on. Nothing short of a sensation! We advance in the Jeeps and, yes, it's a Canadian right-handed Ford with the chassis number C0105159. Right then and there, we believed that the find suddenly increased the number of known LRDG vehicles in Egypt, but later data indicate that the wreck was discovered by Andras Zboray in 2004, and Swedish military vehicle expert Erik Ahlström doubts that the vehicle belonged to the LRDG. Either way, the preserved paint fragments on the wreck contribute to military history, as the color details so far had been scanty. A seemingly small find but of great value for those who want to paint their vehicles with the correct color. After careful studies – we took our time at these amazing places – we continued along the track that was apparently almost untouched since the war. We could also observe that the jerrycans along the track have retained the paint on the sides against the sand. They have probably not been moved for decades.

We reached another wreck, probably one of the vehicles used on the route between Sudan and the Kufra Oasis. They were car models with abilities far below those of the patrol vehicles that LRDG had. We had found a Ford Truck with a so-called waterfall front and a roundel from the Sudan Defense Force or possibly the RAF, the colors were not completely distinguishable.

After lunch we proceeded. I think it would be fair to say that our expedition represents a fairly high concentration of knowledge about equipment, tactics and logistics of the LRDG, a unit with fans in several countries.

Soon we get our first [and only] puncture. We do not arrive as planned at Eight Bells, but actually at another field from where LRDG's two Waco machines could fly wounded to medical treatment. Many flimsies mark the spot. Toby has prepared a real surprise: probably the first flight over the field since 1943! Not with an airplane, but with a kite with a camera, that he controls from the ground with the same kind of remote control used for radio-controlled aircraft. It takes great pictures.

Shortly after we left the airfield we sighted our third truck wreck, also a Ford CMP, but without frame.

We camped a little later at the position N23.04.994, E26.20.529.

Now Toby introduces the rum moment, like the evening rum LRDG received as a kind of compensation for the desolation of the desert and the chilly nights. A bonus for us Westerners, our Muslim friends do not share our delight.

Friday, 13 April

During the morning we had deep sand under the tires, even on flat ground. In spite of this, the Jeeps performed very well in second gear, with four-wheel drive and in some modes low gear and full throttle. The speed was only around 20-30 kilometres per hour, half the normal speed in second gear.

Another wreck appeared, this time one of the LRDG's White 10-tonne transport trucks. Perfect timing beacause it also happened to be lunch time. After some days of eating outside, three meals a day, we have still not found a single grain of sand in our food.

After lunch, it was not far to the next truck, a Chevrolet with a cab that directly disqualified it - Chevrolets in LRDG did not have any unnecessary things like cabins. It had most likely been a work horse on the busy road between Sudan and Kufra and one day it had simply broken down.

After quite a hard drive we approached the legendary place Three Castles, the characteristic peaks that appear a lot in books about the LRDG. Sam then produced a special thing he had made for this place, a brass plaque decorated with poppies (associated with British veterans) to honor the LRDG. A short ceremony ended the assembly, so we were on our way again, chased by our schedule. The evening quickly approached, as did darkness, and neither Mahmud nor Major Sherif was particularly pleased. We were still in a hazardous area and must choose a campsite carefully to get the best protection. Only when the darkness was almost complete, we came to a suitable place.

The military patrol kept guard all night. The expedition members were asked to walk in a certain direction for toilet visits, and only return from the same direction. Anyone approaching the camp is considered to be a potential threat, and the soldiers are quite heavily armed with Kalashnikov assault rifles and a machine gun. Later we will be told that not far from the site were 35 bodies that were thought to be refugees from Darfur or Ethiopia who had attempted to reach Europe via Libya. We also heard that it was not unusual for human traffickers to take refugees to a place in the desert, pointing out a star on the horizon, saying, "There is Tripoli, just walk there, and you will be safe." As Jason Paterniti then put it: "the desert holds great beauty, but also a great measure of sorrow".

The position of the camp was N23.39.033, E25.09.937.

Unlike other places we camped on, the expedition cannot really recommend this place.

Saturday, 14 April

We started the day visiting the Foggini-Mestikawi cave which was discovered as late as 2002. It was close to our camp. The paintings are hard to date, but they are between 5,000 and 9,000 years old, and the quality certainly beats the so-called Swimmers Cave in Wadi Sura, where we arrived a few hours later. The hardcore gang instead checked the tires and the ring pressure, refueled and changed oil filters. Then they switched to field welding of the Army Patrol Land Cruiser's silencer, that was giving up. The welding was done by short-circuiting connected batteries, and Rick came quite far before we had to postpone the project due to the time factor. In front of us we had 90 kilometers driving in rocky terrain, to get to the Aqaba Pass. After an hour's drive we reached the Cave of the Beast, known from the movie "The English Patient".

The day is especially hot. The Ford Jeep´s carburetor has a design that makes it more sensitive to temperature changes than that of the Willys Jeep. When the engine is now knocking it is because the carburettor is too hot, which is countered by tearing apart Ricks shirt, and fastening a piece of it around the carburettor and then adding water to it. When the cloth dries, it draws heat from the carburettor. An old desert trick.

We leave the area around Gilf Kebir and drive to the southern edge of the Great Sand Sea. Our camp has the position N24.02012, E25.59.449.

Sunday, 15 April

The plan today is to take us to a plateau about 15 kilometers from our campsite. Since the plateau has no name, we are going to name the place after Mahmud Marai. This hitherto unexplored plateau in the Gilf Kebir massif is located over 330 kilometers from Dakhla to the east and almost 300 kilometers from Kufra Oasis in Libya to the west.

During the night it was quite windy in our camp, located at the edge of a big sand dune. Just as we broke up, there was a sandstorm far away to the east that darkened the sky above the plateau. We estimated our intended direction in the almost foggy landscape and crossed our fingers that the storm would not really hit us. The mist was sand in the air, but no real storm. Real sandstorms can last for several days if it's bad, and then it's impossible to travel or even cook. You can barely drink.

Once at out destination we stayed in a wadi, LRDG style, and almost the whole gang went off to make discoveries. Jason was very keen to investigate some mysterious roundels he had seen on Google Earth and had no car trails nearby that imply modern activity. Others were keen to discover their very own cave. They are inspired by the Italians who found one in 2002. The cave should preferably have nine thousand year old cave paintings.

John and Toby clean the air filters and change oil in them plus give the Jeeps a little general love.

I myself enjoy a bit of loneliness and go up a hillside where it feels like no one went before, except maybe someone 9,000 years ago. At the same time, I wonder if we really will get to Siwa. It must be said that the expedition has already passed "the point of no return", as pilots put it.

The cave people come back a little disillusioned. No cave. Jason, on the other hand, is lyrical and walks on clouds. The roundes he noticed in Google Earth are most likely watch towers from the fertile period about 9,000 years ago. Now he has seen one of them in real life and up close, at 891 metres above sea level.

We leave the wadi and enter the Great Sand Sea at the point N 24.12.000, E25.60.000 and steer to the north. Because we mainly drive in the kilometre wide corridors between the dunes, the passage is easy and fast at first. Passages in this part of the Sahara/Libyan desert are usually not done along, but across. For example, from Ain Dalla to Big Cairn, LRDG's main route. Or the most common, through tourist expeditions with start and finish in the Siwa Oasis. It is not known that any group has chosen our intended route since the Second World War, and definitely not in veteran vehicles from the war.

The journey continues to the peculiar rock formation Pillar Rock, which is mentioned in LRDG literature, and shortly thereafter, despite the delays, we are on time in the Great Sand Sea. I had thought until now that we were still behind schedule, but we were not. The conscious changes in the program by Gilf Kebir as well as surprisingly good average speed on excellent ground have done the trick.

The Jeeps continue to work well, which also astonishes me a lot because I have had a number of aging cars and always expect cars to cause trouble in one way or another. Out here in the wilderness, the car conditions are particularly difficult, but despite this they roll on. Now the weather begins to become both warmer and windy. We are now starting to be able to "read" the sand and adjust the driving accordingly. Lovely! Distance traveled during this day: 171 kilometres on fantastic ground. We camp at N25.21.726, E25.57.455.

I try to sleep without the tent, dig a long pit in the very loose sand, and lay with an extra sleeping bag to really experience the desert's magnificence, not least the starry sky. Well, the beauty of the desert is somewhat diminished by snores that you do not hear so well in the tent, and the sky is not that fantastic, because I'm so near-sighted that I almost cannot see my own hand without glasses. It will be the only night without a tent.

Monday, 16 April

We have not met a single new person for a whole week. There are not that many places on earth where this is possible.

Our goal this day is, aside from the journey through the Great Sand Sea (a goal in itself), to reach one more known trace of the LRDG, a Ford V8 that is located approximately midway on the trail between Ain Dalla and Big Cairn. The same trail that W Patrol used in early September 1940. We are now mainly going east, meaning that during the day we do no less than eight west-east dune crossings, and I will explain what this means. Untouched sand dunes in the desert are usually so firm that they can carry a car that travels with very low ring pressure if it has some speed and does not swerve too much. A sand dune can either rise softly over the landscape, or be more sharply contoured. Along the dunes you can often drive with rear-wheel drive and at speeds of around 60 kilometres per hour. That is how we mostly drove. But because we were driving north and northwest we had to cross a number of dunes, thus crossing them. Then it becomes more tricky and requires some experience and intuition of the drivers, as well as cold nerves.

Uphill you drive in soft serpentines and the most important thing is to make really long turns so that you do not lose speed. Jason stresses the concept of momentum, that I associate with motion energy. In this case it means making sure you do not lose momentum through a sloppy shift, unnecessary swerve or driving down into someone else's tracks. If you lose momentum, you are suddenly stuck in the sand. As if a giant hand pushed the Jeep down to the wheel axles. But you will hopefully get up without getting stuck. Up there you want to go down the other side of the dune. First, you recognize either by driving along the dune to see if any side is roughly as flat as the one on which it was raised. Or on foot if you consider the surface possible to stop on. Usually, you will find such a side. Otherwise it is easiest, and most exciting, to descend perpendicular to the dune. Something that resembles downhill skiing.

Once you are ready to go down, drive to the edge, put in first gear and slip on the idle at a very steep angle, and just in the bend where the sand is often loose, you give full gas and go forward or slightly upwards and ask for momentum to suffice so you are not caught. Use the four-wheel drive if you have not already done it, and as the last resort, the low gear, this wonderful extra help that can make the Jeep climb up places you cannot dream that a car can get up. But the sand can be worse. If you get stuck beneath a dune it becomes very problematic, and luckily the expedition did not have that problem.

The usual thing when a jeep gets stuck in loose sand is that two or more people use the side handles to pull the Jeep 30-40 meters backwards, where you have come from and there is better ground. Then the driver takes a seat again and in new tracks, maneuvering generally succeeds. But if there is a hundred metre high dune behind, one has to think of something else.

In the evening we arrive at the place where an LRDG vehicle got its last resting place. It is one of the 4x4 V8 Fords that Bagnold reluctantly received in 1941 when the stock of Chevrolet was meagre.

Everything is going well with the driving, everyone gets a turn at the wheel, when the military Toyota in the afternoon gets firmly stuck and must be dug out. This whole car with five people is self-sufficient with camp equipment and gasoline, plus water for the entire journey. With its weapons it is overloaded, and it requires a lot of skill to drive it in loose sand. One of the other Toyotas notices the incident and stops to help, we in the Jeeps do not notice anything but follow the other Toyota that just continues.

After a while we discover that the expedition has been split up, and begin to look for the rear half. At that point eight men have worked furiously for over an hour to get unstuck, and, even though this was unintentional, are pissed off because they have been abandoned. Hard words followed, but in the following morning it was a new day without hard feelings. This was the only open "conflict", which must be pretty good considering that the participants were from four quite different cultures and did not know each other that much. We had now all learnt an important lesson: how fast one can move away from each other, even though everyone has the ambition to hold together. This can lead to serious consequences in the desert, especially when you cannot call someone and lack navigation skills beyond using GPS. The LRDG measured star height and used advanced dead reckoning to know where they were. Then it was about life and death. Numerous are the stories of people who just wanted to go to the toilet at night, and never again were seen.

We drive the Jeeps down the last dune, towards the old Ford, which is in a pit. Photography and surveying takes place. Discussions of origin, about armament, about the disadvantages of this vehicle type. A nice moment before we enjoy the cooked meal in the camp above. Another lovely day.

Today's mileage on varying surfaces was 272 kilometers, and the position of the camp was N26.59.137, E26.34.158.

Tuesday, 17 April

In the morning we headed for a former Russian oil drilling project which instead of oil resulted in - water! As always, the journey there gave a rich experience of the interaction between human and car, and an example of a working relationship between people. During the voyage, the Ford Jeep's clutch joint breaks, and we stay for lunch and repairs. It turns out that the goods are old, one end is very worn, and because we cannot weld, we have to find another solution, and the right one too. Without a good, functional clutch, you are lost in the desert with the fast shifts required in the unsynchronized gearboxes. But the help is close. Tariq quickly fixes a new joiner of a skewer from the kitchen! It's about a millimeter, and he's under the Jeep for half an hour in the sand and adjusts the skewer. Tariq's repair works the whole journey, and according to Toby, there is no need to replace it when the Jeep reached England.

We see nothing but sand that day, and everyone gets ample opportunity to drive 4x4.

When we reached the junk-filled place of the former oil project, the one that became a water project, we were all soon at the permanent water squirt and could clean ourselves properly with water for the first time in a week. A nice experience.

The quite dirty place is not suitable for camps, our now very spoiled expedition thinks. The camp for the night is set up a bit away from the Russian drilling site, at the position N29.10.673, E25.29.466.

A warm *khamseen* blew down from Sudan when I lay on top of the sleeping bag and it was far too hot to get inside it. Fell asleep. But the wind turned, and soon after midnight it became northerly and quite cold. I woke up because I froze. I crept into my sleeping bag and fell asleep. I dreamed that I went into an apartment and slammed the door quite hard after me. Then the room was filled with a low sound, but quite loud, and I felt as if I had started the noise and got a bad conscience. Behind me the door was opened, and my neighbor, a young woman, asked me to look into her apartment. Something mysterious had happened there. I went in, and saw that her entire floor was moving up and down! At the same time, the noise had increased. I promised to call the house janitor. Then I woke up.

The loud sound was still there, in real life, it sounded like a train. I got the flashlight. Through the cloth streamed fine sand horizontally, not only through the zipper, but through the cloth itself. The wind force was incredible, and I realized that if the tent blew apart, my belongings would be in Libya or Chad by the morning. I chucked everything into my backpack, took on my clothes and goggles, pulled my hat over my head and tried to lay down. It was not possible, as the tent had blown around my back. But I could sleep on top of the tent. It went well. Do I need to mention that I am a good sleeper?

In the morning the storm had died down and it became really pleasant. Everybody discussed the night's experiences, giving each other a picture of their little adventure.

If the storm continues for three to four days, which is not uncommon, we'd been in real trouble. You cannot cook, the only thing is to ride out the storm. We were so lucky to just get a shortened version!

Wednesday, 18 April

Desert driving all day. Our last day in the Great Sand Sea and, like the LRDG patrols seventy years ago, we want to get to the Siwa Oasis as soon as possible. Tired but happy. We entered the Desert Rose Hotel, a true desert hotel and under a roof beside there is a 1938 Vauxhall in original condition. Well, almost. We all yearn for a real bed.

Thursday, 19 April

We have a good long morning, I had slept like a king in my single room. After a shower and a longer hygiene procedure, we had a wonderful breakfast in a real building! You appreciate floors, walls, a regular table and comfortable chairs after a week in the desert. Then some telephone conversations with my family and my co-author Lars Gyllenhaal. Even manage to send him a photo for his blog.

Now the flies appear, eager buggers that cannot be wiped away. However, only a pale shadow of the flies that the soldiers testified about during the desert war. In swarms they follow the food, and you do not know where they have been. Or worse: you just *know* where they have been.

After changing oil in the Jeep air filter it's time to really enter Siwa town for a look and to pick up some cash from a wall. The latter not so easy: all credit cards are not accepted, but eventually all get at least some pocket money through deals between with those who have succeeded and others who have dollars. Now we shall explore again. There is only a small crowd of tourists, the Arab spring has meant a sharp decline. We understand that those who live on tourism feel a bit desperate. It is soon general election, and because there are no democratic traditions, the mood is uncertain. The people in Siwa are of a different kind compared to the relatively enlightened middle class with students and business people that you meet on the streets of Cairo. Here, all women and girls over the age of 10 are veiled, and you see almost only men and boys outside.

Not a single camel in sight, on the other hand, many donkeys and donkey carts. As well as three-wheel motorbikes from South Korea. The drivers are not seldom 10 year old boys, and their passengers are often their mother and grandmother. The atmosphere and reception in the small shops was always friendly and not at all intrusive as you often experience in Cairo.

By the way, Siwa has been inhabited at least since the Egyptian 26th dynasty. According to the legend, the Persian king Cambyses II in 525 BC lost his army because it tried to get to Siwa. Not a drop of blood was shed, the brave fifty thousand were buried alive by a sandstorm. There are those who are still looking for traces of them. Tired of it, you can do like us, have a nice meal at the little restaurant "East-West" that beats most restaurants and costs considerably less than expected. Actually we came to Siwa one day early, the plan had been an overnight stay nearby, at a kind of campsite. The plan was overruled. In the evening, we as planned moved into Siwa's first class Paradise Hotel.

Friday, 20 April to Sunday, 22 April

We are early up for the return to Alexandria, a rather uninteresting trip of 560 kilometers. Instead of an ice cold in Alex, we go for an ice cold in Bourg el Arab, and the following day we drive the last stretch, 226 kilometers, to Giza and Mena House hotel, where the expedition ends. In total, according to Jason's calculations, we traveled over 3,769 kilometers, of which 1 591 kilometers in desert terrain.

Reflections

As a preparation for the 2012 desert expedition, I had bought a Willys Jeep CJ2A from 1947. I wanted to match the driving skills of the other expedition members. I was already quite good at the history of the LRDG. How did it go then? When I now reflect on and summarize my experiences the answer is: far beyond my expectations! This was my big Adventure.

But there is more to discover. At the same time as our Jeep expedition was taking place, an intact and unscathed Second World War aircraft wreck, a P-40 Kittyhawk, was found not that far from our route.

I want to finish my diary with the thought of all the discoveries left to be made, not only in the deserts of Egypt but also in other places and in millions of other subjects if you dare to face challenges. Why hesitate? *Who dares wins* (which happens to be the motto of the SAS).

16

'Swede' in the Ghost Patrol

The younger of the two authors of this book (Lars Gyllenhaal) learnt about the LRDG as a teenager in the early 1980s, from a well-used book about SAS founder David Stirling, *The Phantom Major* by Virginia Cowles. Perhaps somewhat strangely, reading a book about David Stirling made me more interested in the LRDG than the SAS, and I am pretty sure that the reason for this was that I could not stop thinking about the LRDG motto, *Non vi sed arte*, Not by strength, by guile, penned by Dr. Francis (Frank) B. Edmundson, LRDG medical officer from the New Zealand Medical Corps.[1] During this period of my teenage years I was actively searching for a philosophy for my life and I thought - and still think today - that the four Latin words *Non vi sed arte* constitute an almost complete philosophy of life, and one that I still try to live by.

The next major inspiration was seeing a particular magazine cover. The year was 1984 and the magazine was the battlefield research journal *After the Battle*. The cover featured a stunning image, a beautiful desert scenery dominated by an amazingly complete wreck of an LRDG Chevrolet, bearing the Maori name of "Waikaha". It was in an unexpectedly well-preserved state as it was found after standing untouched for forty years.

After seeing that cover photo my daydreaming, especially during endless math classes, was usually about going to North Africa and traveling through the desert in an open vehicle. I was lucky enough to get to know a guy who was a little older than me, who was also an LRDG enthusiast and who owned an original 1943 Ford Jeep, a vehicle that theoretically may once have been part of the Ghost Patrol. We talked about making a trip in the tracks of the LRDG and for this purpose I obtained maps and tourist brochures from several kind North African diplomats in Stockholm.

We then never got to North Africa, but at least we drove with my friend's Jeep from Stockholm to Wales, on a kind of pilgrimage to see the great relic from that cover photo, "Waikaha", which at this time, 1986, was still preserved in a Welsh cave. With a view to the moisture I guess the place was not ideal, so a protective room had been constructed around "Waikaha".

The word pilgrimage perfectly reflects how I regarded the Chevrolet that came home from the desert. I wrote the following words in my photo album under the picture of it: "The lost son has returned".

A year earlier, I had somehow received the address of the LRDG Association, then still run by LRDG veterans, and after several years of correspondence with the extremely helpful secretary Jim Patch, he advised me that a former patrolman with the nickname 'Swede' recently had let the association know of his postwar life and whereabouts. Within the LRDG Association, all they had known about William 'Swede' Anderson was that he went missing in action in January 1942. He had been with G1 Patrol escorting a SAS team under the command of David Stirling, the phantom major himself, to the Libyan coastal town of Buerat. The last thing his comrades had seen of Anderson was that he sought shelter during a bomb attack out in the desert, in Wadi Tamet.

---

1   Gross, p. 19.

I wrote to Anderson, who in 1988 lived in Nottingham, and received a reply from his wife because he was then not in shape to write himself. But a few months later he did write to me. To summarize what Pat and Bill Anderson told me, 'Swede' was actually of Swedish-Norwegian extraction, but he had become known as 'Swede' because he matched all the expectations of the 1940s about how a Swedish man should look like: tall, fit and blonde with blue eyes. The photo I received from him did not disappoint, the man was a Viking. He had become a professional soldier in the Scots Guards in 1938. From his time with the LRDG he could find no photographs, but, in 2012 I got a picture from his Ghost Patrol days, thanks to the Long Range Desert Group Preservation Society (more photographs were later sent to me from his living relatives).

After basic military training, Swede Anderson had been sent to Egypt. He had already been in the country for some time and had adapted to it, when the war broke out. He was one of the first men to report his interest in joining the newly established LRPU, which later became LRDG. He wrote to me that it was basically thirst for adventure that motivated him, and that he might have been inspired by his father who saw both the Arctic and sailed around Cape Horn as a sailor. However, Swede was not immediately allowed to transfer from the Scots Guards, he had to wait until the summer of 1941.

In LRDG, Swede first got to drive a Chevrolet truck. He recalled that "the Chevs had took a bashing on the previous jobs at Murzuk and Kufra", to quote from one of his letters.

Anderson had been in Kufra for a short time and then placed in Siwa. He became very fond of his new unit and thought he experienced the magnificence of nature much like the polar explorer Shackleton and mountaineer Mallory, two men who Anderson admired during his youth.

From Siwa Oasis, Anderson drove off on various missions and it happened that he also shot at the enemy. Particularly one mission was bloody, only six of eighteen men in the patrol were not injured. About his very last patrol he wrote a bit more to me:

> When my truck was blown up we were separated from the rest of the patrol [...] We marched by the north star at night [...] We were in a terrible state when we were captured, we were licking water from the rims of oil barrels when the Germans got us. We were too weak to put up our hands. Another two days I think we would have perished.[2]

The fighting was over for Swede and he was sent to a prisoner of war camp south of Naples and then on to Germany.

When Swede looked back on his life, the time in LRDG was nevertheless a highlight:

> We were a motley crew far removed from the spit and polish of the Guards, our RSMs [regimental sergeant majors] would have thrown fits if they had seen us, but we were a great crowd. I will never forget my days in the LRDG, I loved the desert although I could have died there.[3]

For his war service, Swede received four medals. The medal he seemed to value most was his Africa Star. As such, it was not that special, all from the British Commonwealth who had seen operational service in North Africa got it, but it was apparently the time in North Africa, and especially when he was with the LRDG, that was the light for Anderson during the dark war years.

2   Letter from William Anderson to Lars Gyllenhaal dated 5 May 1988, in the LRDG collection of Gyllenhaal.
3   Ibid.

Bill "Swede" Anderson in Egypt while waiting to go on a practice run with the LRDG, Bill is sitting with his arms folded.
(Peter Anderson and David Hall)

Anderson in the "small" shorts of the British Army.
(Peter Anderson and David Hall)

Bill "Swede" Anderson in Egypt, standing at the back with two friends, Boot and Brown. (Peter Anderson and David Hall)

Bill "Swede" Anderson of G Patrol, in the bottom row, third from the left. Immediately to the right of him, in a peaked cap, is Scots Guards Captain Michael Crichton-Stuart, who formed G Patrol. (LRDG Preservation Society)

Like myself, Swede had gone to Wales to see the well-preserved "Waikaha" and, as his wife Pat wrote to me, "Bill was very thrilled, because it was exactly the same as Bill used to drive".[4]

This contact with Bill Anderson in Nottingham was a great thing for me as a young man, and increased my growing interest in Swedes on the various battlefields of the World Wars – I came to write a book about them. In spite of Sweden declaring itself neutral, no fewer than 23,000 Swedish citizens went to war between 1914 and 1945. Only about 200 joined the Germans in 1939–1945. In the same period more than 1,500 Swedish citizens joined the US Army, and several hundred donned Norwegian, British and French and uniforms. In addition, over 8,000 Swedish sailors transported weapons, fuel etc in Allied convoys, and well over 200,000 men of Swedish descent (either born in Sweden or with Swedish parents) served in the US, British, Canadian, and Australian Armed Forces.

I also became aware of the fact that the LRDG had anti-tank guns from Swedish Bofors. In total, the British Army ordered 250 of them and 80 could be delivered before the war broke out. This was not a significant amount, but there were many more, several thousands, of the famous Bofors anti-aircraft gun in British and US units. One can even say that Bofors guns were a backbone in the air defense system of the Allies. During the battles for El Alamein, Bofors guns firing tracer ammunition played an important role in creating "light corridors" through German minefields.

Guns aside, it was contact with veterans like Bill Anderson, which made me really want to write military history. Thanks to Karl-Gunnar Norén, I finally got the chance to realize my old idea to write more about Anderson and the LRDG.

---

4   Letter from Pat Anderson to Lars Gyllenhaal dated 28 February 1988, in the LRDG collection of Gyllenhaal.

17

The Ghost Patrol recipe

Several books have been published in English about British special forces in North Africa during the Second World War, and in recent years a more critical attitude towards them has also emerged. Were they, and especially LRDG, really as amazing and of such importance as many have claimed?

To begin with, a linguistic remark. Several units during the Second World War, including the LRDG and SAS, were at the time only rarely designated as special forces (or special operations forces). But in modern literature they are often called that. During the war, it was more common to call them saboteurs, special services, private armies and raiders. Nevertheless, the desert war of 1940-43 was the starting point for today's special forces units. Why did they appear so clearly within the British Armed Forces, starting in 1940? The main explanation is perhaps the embarrassing British defeats of 1940 in Norway, France and Greece. After these catastrophic events some asked themselves if there was no smart, unexpected and inexpensive way of weakening the enemy. How about something radically different to then orthodox British military thinking? Surely, there was nothing to lose in fielding small, bold units behind enemy lines?

The LRDG commanding officer from 1943, Major General David Lloyd Owen, praised LRDG founder Ralph Bagnold's basic principles for desert voyages, which Owen thought were also the best recipe for small units planning to operate behind enemy lines. Owen stated that Bagnold's four basic principles were, in his order:

The most careful and detailed planning
First-class equipment
A sound and simple communication system
A human element of rare quality[1]

For more of Lloyd Owen's insights you really should read his excellent war memoirs *The Long Range Desert Group 1940-1945: Providence Their Guide*. Then read Kennedy Shaw's *Long Range Desert Group*.

LRDG showed, in a short space of time, that by stealthily moving through remote and desolate areas and establishing observation posts far behind enemy lines, one could deliver a stream of valuable information about the enemy. If necessary, the same unit could also perform direct action such as attacks against petrol dumps, airfields and outposts. Such actions could, however, counteract intelligence gathering, that often was more important. Thus patrolmen might not fire a single shot during several weeks of operations.

When large formations were preparing for a major offensive, LRDG could instead take on the role of pathfinders. They were well suited for this due to their incredibly good terrain knowledge and navigation specialists.

---

1   Lloyd Owen, p. 5.

A more unexpected value of LRDG was that they were so talented and helpful teachers that they could assist other, fledgling, special forces units to get started and not least transport them to and from their area of operations. From a catastrophic start, with many killed and injured during practice accidents, the early SAS was fortunate enough to be intimately connected with the LRDG. Thanks to LRDG experience, "taxi services" and navigation expertise, the SAS was initially able to concentrate on blowing up particularly important targets, such as aircraft on the ground. The final score for the SAS during the desert war was about 350 destroyed enemy aircraft, which made it possible to compare the effectiveness of the SAS with an air force. Even though direct action was not the primary task of the LRDG, it on occasion (even before there was a SAS) demonstrated that it too could attack airfields with similar results.

Has nothing been exaggerated then? Well, perhaps one thing; the originality of what the SAS founder David Stirling did. Much of what still is most associated with Stirling and the SAS had been developed by LRDG. Some writers forget that the SAS often also relied on the active support of the LRDG. Who's to blame for the excesses and missing facts? Well, not David Stirling. In fact, Stirling tried to draw attention away from his own person, like when he said about his friend and colleague Jock Lewes, "Jock could far more genuinely claim to be the founder of the SAS than I."[2]

However, one thing that is sometimes emphasized about the LRDG is not unambiguous. It has been alleged that Rommel said about the LRDG that they caused the German Armed Forces "more damage than any other British unit of equal strength".[3] But even though Rommel most probably was talking about the SAS, the LRDG can take part of the credit, as the SAS to a great extent started with inspiration and help from the LRDG and then operated largely with the support of LRDG.

LRDG received a clearer rating from Rommel's deputy Ritter von Thoma, who, when captured, made it clear that Montgomery knew more about the logistics of the Germans than he himself did! Most of Monty's knowledge stemmed from LRDG patrols.

The LRDG really maintained a consistent and high quality. The unit personnel strength peaked at 350 men, but in spite of that, between 26 December 1940 and 10 April 1943, only 15 days passed without a patrol being behind or on the flanks of the enemy. Equally remarkable: during the entire desert war 18 men died in LRDG service (not all due to enemy action). Talking about "just 18" is wrong, but it is impossible to ignore the fact that relatively seen this was a very low figure, testifying to how skilled the patrolmen were.

It is therefore difficult not to agree with the following words by Major General Julian Thompson, who commanded 3 Commando Brigade during the Falklands War, from his book *War Behind Enemy Lines*:

Theirs was a yardstick by which one should gauge those [i.e. special forces] that came after them. The LRDG needed adventurous spirits, but never tolerated "cowboys". They were utterly reliable. If they said that they would arrive at an exact spot in the desert 1,000 miles away at a certain time, they almost invariably did. […] They made their radios work over long distances. They got the messages through. This demanded high standards of driving, maintenance and navigation. This was the legacy of Bagnold and the early members of the LRDG: a capacity for taking pains; of thinking the problem through; an intellectual rather than what we would now call a "gung-ho" approach.[4]

2   Andrew L. Hargreaves, *Special Operations in World War II: British and American Irregular Warfare* (Norman: University of Oklahoma Press, 2013), p. 62.
3   Gordon, pp. 185-186.
4   Thompson, p. 33.

18

From LRDG to SAS and Mars!

Both the LRDG and SAS were dissolved during the second half of 1945. An undercover SAS cell remained though, to hunt down and bring to justice the Germans responsible for murdering captured comrades. The SAS was then officially re-established in 1947[1]. Why the SAS but not the LRDG? The desert part of the name may of course be blamed, but names can be changed. More importantly, during 1944 and 1945 the LRDG was largely integrated into the growing and politically more well-positioned SAS (e.g. Churchill's son Randolph had served with the SAS).

The LRDG-SAS integration was quite visible after the Desert War, when SAS berets and SAS jump wings were introduced in the LRDG.

After the LRDG's own veteran association was closed down (due to natural causes), the memory of the LRDG is officially preserved by the SAS Regimental Association.

The Ghost Patrol thus remains within SAS culture, and, on a more physical level, also in the operational SAS mobility troops, the specialists in using vehicles, not least in desert environments. When you see these chaps in the desert from a distance they look an awful lot like a typical LRDG patrol back in 1941.

For desert travelers and special forces units all over the world, the LRDG will probably never stop providing valuable lessons, as several of their tricks will hardly ever be superseded by technological advances.

Brigadier Ralph Bagnold's outstanding desert knowledge also lives on in more unexpected places. His book *The Physics of Blown Sand and Desert Dunes*, published in 1941, has been used by NASA for studying sand dunes on Mars. In fact, a dune field on Mars is since 2015 known as the Bagnold Dunes – the first active dune field to have been explored on another planet (by a car–sized roving laboratory called Curiosity).[2] Ralph Bagnold would probably have been more than pleased by this, as one can deduce from his autobiography *Sand, Wind & War*, published in 1991 (a year after his death), that he was more interested in science than military matters.

Non vi sed arte.

---

1   A still rather unknown part of SAS history, well told by Damien Lewis in his book *Nazi Hunters* (London: Quercus, 2016).

2   Imperial College London, Science: News <https://www.imperial.ac.uk/news/173278/nasa-studies-martian-sand-dunes-named/> (accessed 30 November 2018).

Bibliography

In addition to the sources below, mention should be made of correspondence with Y Patrol veteran James D. Patch, secretary of the Long Range Desert Group Association, as well as G Patrol veteran William "Swede" Anderson. The letters from them are in Lars Gyllenhaal's personal archive. Of importance to the book was also an essay by Andrew L. Hargreaves entitled 'The Advent, Evolution and Value of British Specialist Formations in the Desert War 1940-43', which appeared in the journal *Global War Studies* 7 (2) 2010. In addition, we have been inspired by some very old but still good desert war films such as 'Sea of Sand' and 'Ice Cold in Alex', both of which are from 1958. Especially 'Sea of Sand' is worth watching because it is about the LRDG on the eve of Alamein. Y Patrol is given the task of blowing up a major petrol dump and what follows feels hot and rather gritty. The film was shot on location in Libya and the film's technical advisor was none other than Bill Kennedy Shaw, the LRDG intelligence officer.

Archives:
The most important LRDG archive is preserved by Churchill College, Cambridge. Karl-Gunnar Norén there studied the relevant 32 capsules on the structure of the LRDG, its operations and Ralph Bagnold's personal documents, photographs and letters, all deposited by the National Archives at the Churchill Archives Centre at Churchill College. The collection is to be found under the designation Ralph Bagnold (BGND) and NCUACS35.3.92/C.1 - C.32.

The following archives/museums have helped us with photographs: Churchill Archives Centre, The Royal Signals Museum, The Alexander Turnbull Library at the National Library of New Zealand, Archives New Zealand.

Books:
Asher, Michael, *Get Rommel* (London: Cassell, 2005).

Bagnold, Ralph, *Sand, Wind, and War: Memoirs of a Desert Explorer* (Tucson: University of Arizona Press, 1991).
Bagnold, Ralph, *Libyan Sands: Travel in a Dead World* (London: Eland, 2010).
Beaton, Cecil & Buckle, Richard, *Self portrait with friends: the selected diaries of Cecil Beaton, 1926-1974* (New York: The New York Times Book Company, 1982).
Broberg, Jan, *Flygande tigrar och ökenråttor* (Staffanstorp: Bo Cavefors Bokförlag, 1970).

Connor, Ken, *Ghost Force: The Secret History of the SAS* (London: Cassell, 1998).
Cowles, Virginia, *The Phantom Major* (London: The Companion Book Club, 1958).
Crichton-Stuart, Michael, *G Patrol* (London: William Kimber, 1958).

Ford, Ken, *The Mareth Line 1943* (2012) (Oxford: Osprey, 2012).

Gordon, John W., *The Other Desert War: British Special Forces in North Africa, 1940-1943* (Westport: Praeger, 1987).

Goudie, Andrew, *Wheels Across the Desert* (Broadstairs: Silphium Press, 2008).

Gross, Kuno with Chiarvetto, Roberto and O'Carroll, Brendan, *Incident at Jebel Sherif* (Singapore: Star Standard Industries Ltd, 2009).

Gyllenhaal, Lars & Westberg, Lennart, *Swedes at War: Willing Warriors of a Neutral Nation* (Bedford: The Aberjona Press, 2010).

Hargreaves, Andrew L., *Special Operations in World War II: British and American Irregular Warfare* (Norman: University of Oklahoma Press, 2013).

Hoe, Alan, *David Stirling* (London: Warner Books, 1994).

Jenner, Robin & List, David, *The Long Range Desert Group* (London: Osprey Publishing Ltd., 1985).

Kelly, Saul, *The Lost Oasis: The True Story Behind The English Patient* (Boulder: Westview Press, 2003).

Kennedy Shaw, W.B., *Long Range Desert Group: The story of its work in Libya* (London: Collins, 1945).

Ladd, James D., *SAS Operations* (London: Robert Hale, 1986).

Lewis, Damien, *Nazi Hunters* (London: Quercus, 2016).

Lloyd Owen, David, *The Desert My Dwelling Place* (London: Arms and Armour Press, 1957).

Lloyd Owen, David, *Providence Their Guide: The Long Range Desert Group 1940-1945* (Barnsley: Pen & Sword, 2000).

Maclean, Fitzroy, *Eastern Approaches* (London: The Reprint Society, 1951).

Moreman, Tim, *Long Range Desert Group Patrolman* (Oxford: Osprey Publishing Ltd, 2010).

Morgan, Mike, *Sting of the Scorpion* (Stroud, The History Press, 2010).

Mortimer, Gavin, *The Men Who Made the SAS* (London: Constable, 2015:1).

Mortimer, Gavin, *Stirling's Desert Triumph* (Oxford: Osprey, 2015:2).

Mortimer, Gavin, *The Long Range Desert Group in World War II* (Oxford: Osprey, 2017).

Norén, Karl-Gunnar, *Tobruk. Australiensarna som hejdade Rommel* (Stockholm: Nielsen & Norén Förlag, 2011).

Norén, Karl-Gunnar, *El Alamein 1942* (Stockholm: Nielsen & Norén Förlag, 2005).

O'Neill, Herbert Charles, *The tide turns* (London: Faber and Faber, 1944).

Peniakoff, Vladimir, *Popski's Private Army* (London: The Reprint Society, 1953).

Sadler, John, *Ghost Patrol. A History of the Long Range Desert Group, 1940–1945* (Oxford: Casemate, 2015).

Special Forces in the Desert War 1940-43 (Kew: The National Archives, 2008).

Swinson, Arthur, *The Raiders* (London: Macdonald & Co, 1969).

Timpson, Alastair & Gibson-Watt, Andrew, *In Rommel's Backyard* (Barnsley: Pen & Sword Military, 2000).

Thompson, Julian, *War Behind Enemy Lines* (London: Sidgwick & Jackson, 1998).

Vanderveen, Bart, 'Desert Chevrolets: A lone Long Range Desert Group survivor and its contemporaries', *Wheels & Tracks* No. 8 (July 1984), pp. 14-21.

Whiting, Charles, *Hitlers hemliga krig. Tredje rikets spioner* (Stockholm: Fischer & Co, 2010).

Whittaker, Len, *Some Talk of Private Armies* (Harpenden: Albanium Publishing, 1984).

Wynter, H.W, *The History of the Long Range Desert Group* (Singapore: The National Archives, 2008).

Index

Index of Places

Index of Operations